# Praise for

# Bill's Im-Perfect Time Management Adventure

"Finally! An engaging story about time management with flesh-and-blood characters. Bill's Im-Perfect Time Management Adventure reads like a suspense novel. You'll hardly know you're learning the most organic and flexible system for managing your time that exists." Judith Kolberg, author *Getting Organized in the Era of Endless: What To Do When Information, Interruptions and Work is Endless and Time is Not*

"Francis is unique because he has not only come up with a good time management system for himself, but he has then gone on to dissect what works and then present it to the world in a format other people can directly apply without any prior knowledge. Yaro Starak, *Entrepreneurs-Journey.com*

"Substantial productivity tips packed up and rolled into a superb novel." Leon Ho, founder of *Lifehack*

# Bill's Im-Perfect Time Management Adventure

## A Business Fable

Francis Wade

Bill's Im-Perfect Time Management Adventure - A Business Fable
Francis Wade

Copyeditor: Ellen Fishbein
Cover art: iStockphoto
Cover design by Jasmin jw12792 on fiverr.com

First edition: February 2013

Published in the United States by 2Time Labs Press
ISBN 978-1-482-38634-9

This book is available for bulk purchases, at a special discount.

The education you need is within you. How can what is already within you be taught? It can only be realized. If you're willing to go inside and wait for the truth, your inborn wisdom meets the questions, and the answer rings true as if it were a tuning fork inside your own being.

The best way of leading people is to let them find their own way.

Byron Katie

# Table of Contents

# Preface

I could blame this all on Eli Goldratt. He's the author of *The Goal: A Process of Ongoing Improvement*, a book on optimizing factory production.

Between semesters as a Cornell graduate student in 1988, I worked at AT&T Bell Labs, commuting each week from New Jersey to their Shreveport Works in Louisiana. Someone recommended the book, written in the form of a business fable, and I started to read it over lunch.

I could barely put it down.

In a few short hours, it taught me more about real life factory operations than anything I had studied in four years of Ivy League education in operations research and industrial engineering.

I was stunned. How could a simple story be so effective?

Fast forward to 2009 and my commitment to develop the principles of Time Management 2.0 into a form that anyone could recognize and use. Blogs, online training, videos, podcasts, Facebook pages and tweets were all useful, but too many people, particularly those in less developed countries, saw these as exotic channels for privileged geeks.

The sample chapter I wrote in March of that year looks amusing today, but it represents my first, flawed effort to turn abstract principles into a full story. Goldratt made it look so easy.

That brings us to what I now call "The Bill Book" - the document you are now reading on a screen or on paper. Well established principles underlie this tale. I know that some will undoubtedly skip the story of Bill, Sandy, Vernon and Martha and head straight to the back pages, where I have listed the principles of Time Management 2.0 and links to a buffet of learning opportunities.

That's not a problem. In fact, that's the point. Take charge of this learning experience and use it to enhance your life in a way that works for you.

Good luck on this journey. As you'll see, you've been on it for a long time - long before you ever heard about *Bill's Im-Perfect Time Management Adventure.* I hope that this book will illuminate the pathway that brought you to your current methods and guide you to chart a course to the promised land. You can manage your time and proactively change your methods as your needs evolve.

Unfortunately, Eli Goldratt passed away during the writing of this book. The following quotation from his book, *The Choice*, inspires me today: "Every situation, no matter how complex it initially looks, is exceedingly simple."

Francis

2Time Labs
http://perfect.mytimedesign.com

# Chapter 1

"More Layoffs Expected in New Jersey."

The headline from the Sunday New York Times screamed at me from the front page, sending a single, distinct chill down my spine.

Shifting in my seat, I struggled to take some deep breaths to push down the tightening of my gut. It had nothing to do with flight AA 345, hurtling through the air on the way back to Newark from Shreveport via Dallas on a warm June afternoon. I removed the paper from the seat pocket in front of me and then flipped it around to hide the headline. My hand shook, and I tried to steady it so the lady sitting next to me wouldn't notice.

I tried to convince my mind to ignore the email I had received earlier that week. *It's anonymous. Might not be real.* That didn't seem to work, so I closed my eyes to try to force myself to sleep, but the image popped right back like a bad tune that just wouldn't go away.

===========================
**Unknown**
-------------------------------------------------
From: Unknown<Stevnellie9612@aol.com>
To: Bill.Crossley@syscon.com
Subject: FYI - Urgent

See below ********-//////-VVVVV

From: Manuel.Bonares@syscon.com
To: Martha.Adelman@syscon.com, ManagersTeam@syscon.com
Subject: Keep this private

Here is the list -- please keep this extremely quiet. These are the employees / Project Managers who the executives feel are our weakest. Mostly, they are looking at their productivity / reliability / time management skills, and whether or not they are getting overwhelmed by everything they have to do.

< Bill, I cut out the other names.>

- Bill Crossley, Project Manager, New Education Technologies Group

The VP's will let us know what to do next, so don't panic - this is a preliminary list. As you know, we have been overstaffed at the Project Manager level for some time, so it's only logical that this level will be the one that we tackle next.

Manuel

-----------------------------------------------

I thought of my boss Martha. Knowing her hatred of confrontation, I thought, *she must be wetting her pants*. She was probably suffering as much as I was.

Or maybe I was the only one suffering.

*It isn't fair*. I deserved to keep my job. I had worked hard to put in long hours. But the results were now staring me in the face.

*Are my time management skills that bad?*

I glared at the seat in front of me as the plane made its final descent. The flight attendant gave out muffled instructions –blah, blah, blah - I had heard it a million times before, but all I could think about was how to turn this around. Sandy and the kids, plus Mom and Dad. They all depended on me.

And who the hell was Stevnellie9612@aol.com? Was it Joseph?

Poor guy. He was "restructured" just before Christmas last year, according to Ted, my colleague and ally in our division at Syscon. Now, he clocked in at the Starbucks on Alphonso Street every day, in his work clothes and with his briefcase. The rumor mill had it that his wife didn't have a clue that her family was now living on dwindling savings and his unemployment. He simply hadn't told her that he'd been fired. He was desperately trying to find something before funds ran out (or one of her friends ran into him on a latte run).

Did he send me the heads up? That didn't seem to fit, because the tone of the email wasn't friendly and there was no longer a reason for him to hide anything. I felt another cold chill. Would there be another mysterious email waiting for me in the office?

The napkin in my hands was now damp, even though the cabin was dry and cold enough to make my sinuses rasp.

"It just isn't fair," I grunted softly to myself.

Martha had dropped the first bomb on Tuesday morning, shortly before I left town and before the email had arrived. "Upper management" needed to cut "a few" more people to make its budget, and they had to identify the weakest staff members, especially at the Project Management level. My level. The information confirmed what the email said, but she had left out the part about my name being on the list.

"Their damned numbers" I spat, a little too loudly this time. Good thing the lady beside me was now dozing, oblivious to my low muttering.

Just a few minutes ago, she had been wide awake, flashing me a cute smile brightened by impossibly perfect teeth.

"I'm from South Yorkshire," she explained in an accent that explained why something felt strangely familiar.

"So are my grandparents!" I shot back with a happy smile. It was all enough to get her to glance at my ring finger before continuing with a joke about folks from that part of England. We laughed together for a few minutes as I shared a few sharp memories, warts and all. Granny and Grandpa were real salt of the earth people from a town she knew well.

When she relaxed into a deep sleep, my mind picked up where it left off. It still didn't feel fair.

Once again, I made a mental list of all the projects I was working on and the number of roles I was filling. The biggest one was the DAPE Project, which I'd been working on for over three years. DAPE was initiated by the executives of Syscon to harmonize a number of e-Learning courses that sat on several platforms across the company. It was a massive cleanup effort, undertaken to resolve a number of conflicting techniques.

Now, I had that job plus two others. *How did that happen?* First, there was the vacancy created two years ago when Anna was seconded to a company in California. Apparently, once it was all over, she'd received a letter asking her not to return to Syscon. Joseph was forced out to take up his new seat at the local Starbucks a year later. That left me to do their jobs as well as my own, and I worked longer days and weekends just to keep up. Now, my job was on the line for the very first time. My fists tightened, and I wondered, "What would I tell Sandy? What would I tell my kids?"

My jacket felt tight around my chest, and I shifted positions. In my lap lay a book I had picked up in the airport bookstore. The title leapt off the page: *2,002 Tips and Tricks in Time Management - Every Shortcut on the Planet!* It was bright yellow with hot red lettering and had the look of a cheap tabloid newspaper. I hadn't been looking for a book to purchase - I mostly bought eBooks - but this one was sitting beside the Times, and it seemed to offer some immediate help.

I was partway through it and opened back up to "Tip #450 - Get up Early." *Pure crud.* With a weary shake of my head, I closed the book for the last time and hid it behind the Times. It was a never-ending list of trivial bits and pieces that offered little more than titillation. *What nonsense.* And, supposedly, a New York Times Bestseller.

Whom was this written for? –The answer was obvious: *tired-out project managers who were scared of being laid off because of their sorry-ass time management skills.* My own stupid joke made me smile a bit. It faded when I remembered that I needed a real solution to this problem. Okay, so chasing down a bunch of tips and hoping for a short-term fix wouldn't work. *What the hell would?*

I glanced at the in-flight monitor overhead. It was 5:00 p.m. Right about now, Lizzy and Rebecca were probably playing in the living room, lost as usual in a game involving long legged Barbies and bright yellow monster trucks. Lizzy liked to pretend that Barbie modeled by day and pulled a night shift driving heavy trucks, which kept Rebecca laughing, even though she was less than a year old. I didn't think that I needed a son with the tough little girls I was raising. What they didn't know was that Sandy and I desperately needed to refinance our mortgage in order to keep that living room.

Like many of other people, we were stuck with one of those ARM mortgage payments that increased dramatically early in the prior year. We applied for a new loan at the local bank, but they told us we needed to put up more cash. We were saving as much as we could, thinking that it might take about a year to hit the targeted amount. In the meantime, the payments kept increasing every quarter, putting a further strain on our finances.

Losing the job would mean... The thought of losing our home made my eyes well up. I blinked hard, fighting back the anger bubbling inside. Every time I imagined something bad happening to the kids I got pissed. Realizing I was the one who had caused it... well, that only made it worse.

Amazingly, I hadn't even thought about Martha, Syscon or anything about my situation since I fell asleep on the flight to Shreveport last Tuesday. I had been going, going, going since then and had done nothing but meet, sleep, talk, listen and travel until today, Sunday. Those few days of being too busy to think about that email had felt like a vacation from my situation.

When my plane landed with a bump at 6 p.m. I felt that little release of tension that comes from being on the ground, so I brightened a bit. It was Sunday, after all. I was heading home to Sandy and the kids, straight to my easy chair in the living room. I'd be able to turn on the TV while trying again to forget.

There was no way I could tell Sandy. This was too damned big for her to handle; one stressed-out Crossley was one too many. *No depressing news.*

At the carousels, I called Carruther's - the limo company – only to find that my driver was delayed for an hour. Only slightly pissed off, I decided that there were worse things than being stuck in Newark airport, the so-called "armpit of America," on a Sunday night.

To kill time, I headed to the bar in Terminal C. A beer would help, I decided. Then, maybe, I could see if the I.T. guys had the patch ready. A virus had wreaked havoc on Outlook, leaving me unable to access my messages for the entire trip. I.T. sent me a text message on Saturday letting me know that there was a patch I could download via the company website, but now I had a new problem. My battery, which should have been replaced months ago, had lost its charge. The charger was in the drawer of my cubicle in the office. I'd have to borrow one.

With my laptop and carry-on in hand, I glanced around slowly, looking for an open stool in the dimly lit, sticky-floored room. I chose a worn out stool in the corner that had borne the weight of too many travelers for too many years. I struggled to balance myself on a cushion that felt as if it were built for a teenager, and I wheeled my stuff into the space between the stool and the wall.

Forgetting about the beer, I ordered a Screwdriver and asked around for a charger. I got lucky on the fifth beg, and I reminded myself that a great business trip was built on small victories just like this.

Within a few minutes, Syscon's servers someplace in Kansas flooded 456 new messages into my email Inbox, courtesy of the Wi-Fi network. 456. On Sunday. We were only a little 1000-person technology firm that offered e-Learning platforms, not the army, but the workload felt like we were about to launch Desert Storm.

My Tzinbox score was -5, on a scale of -10 to +10. The program's warning lights flashed an angry red to tell me I was probably in big trouble. The software was an optional add-on that we used to determine how close we were to the ideal - the Zero Inbox. Not everyone used it, but I liked being on top of things by working through all my incoming email in one go so that it left the Inbox clear and empty. Usually, I had all green lights.

Now, my indicators were all going crazy - the age of the oldest message and the average age of each message were higher than I had ever seen them. But I didn't need the program to tell me how things were going. I knew I was in trouble. Even though I liked "being on top of things," it told me a sad fact. I hadn't achieved a Zero inbox for an entire week in over a year.

I muttered quietly to myself as I desperately glanced through the list of subject lines and senders, hoping that I was looking at a ton of Spam rather than legitimate stuff. Wishful thinking. Three meager pieces of junk mail had escaped the filters, but I was looking at many hours of work just to get back on track. And, to make matters worse, there was an all-day staff retreat planned for Monday.

Completely forgotten. *How did I miss that?*

The tension returned to my shoulders before it spread to my neck and into the small, weak spots in my back. I wished that I had taken a seat at one of the booths so that I could lean back and close my eyes. To get rid of the tight feeling, I stretched upwards on the stool and pulled my arms behind me in a weak imitation of the warm-up I used to do before high-school swimming workouts.

I knew these messages meant several days of long evenings and early mornings, trying to catch up. A week of living in hope that I didn't miss anything important. A half a month of stress.

Sandy hated when I brought work home instead of paying attention to the family, but tonight had to be an exception. Closing down my laptop, I decided that I was too tired to focus on all that email. Instead, I picked up some bits and pieces of the New Jersey Herald, the Washington Post, and US News and World Report as I finished my drink.

Outside on the sidewalk, several hundred tired travelers all had the same look on their faces and probably the same thought in mind: "What am I doing at the airport on a warm, Sunday evening? There was still plenty of light out, and jackets and ties loosened and came off.

---

Standing next to me, a younger guy clicked furiously away at his BrainPhone. He didn't look up once as he hailed his limo, gave the driver his bags, and sat in the back seat. He had a few words with the driver before the vehicle drove off. He didn't look up once. I smiled. It was a piece of well-rehearsed business-traveler ballet. But, not for the first time, I began to think that he was doing a better job with his smartphone than I was doing with my laptop and cell phone combined.

When my driver from Carruthers finally showed up, I slid into the backseat and settled down for a boring ride home, wishing that I could also spend the travel time dealing with email. As I stared out at the landscape of bright, metallic chemical factories, I sniffed the air and then wrinkled my nose. It all helped to make Newark such a charming airport, I thought, when the subject line of an email popped into my mind.

==========================
**Martha Adelman**
-----------------------------------------------
From: Martha Adelman
To: DapeTeam@syscon.com, Directors@syscon.com
Subject: SRD Project Delayed.
-----------------------------------------------

I gasped as we turned onto the ramp for the Turnpike. I tried hard to remember. *Did I tell Martha that the project received new funding? She should never have sent that email. Did she copy anyone in senior management on the message?* My pulse raced as my mind feverishly went over all the nasty things that could happen if she had.

My weakly charged laptop was stuffed in the trunk with the rest of my stuff, so all I could do on the ride home to Piscataway was hope that I hadn't screwed up.

*I need to do better.*

The email and the conversation with Martha - these were real. If I kept losing track...

Ever since Joseph left, I had been forgetting to do all sorts of things at work and at home. Shouldn't that be expected when an employee, even a good one, is forced to do so many jobs at once?

Sandy had noticed and gotten upset with me more than a few times. The worst was when I arrived over an hour late to pick up Lizzy from school. Now, at work, I was rumored to be a weak member of the team.

Locking my jaws, I told myself that I needed to make sure that this SRD bullstuff didn't get me fired, no matter what. This recession was no time to be messing around at work, especially when layoffs were on the horizon. If I wasn't serious before, I needed to get focused now, before I ended up with a promotion to the Starbucks branch of Syscon.

*But where the heck should I start?*

* * *

It was still light outside when my limo pulled up in front of our home on Wentworth Road just after 8 p.m. As we turned the corner into the development and I got my first glimpse of our house, I felt a tiny glow of pride. Sandy and I owned a 4-bedroom colonial in Piscataway - about 30-40 minutes drive from the airport, depending on the traffic. It was painted white with black shutters, which really stood out from the neighbors' houses. I had painted them myself and they looked pretty, overlooking hedges with purple flowers right beside a solid white picket fence.

Our home wasn't the biggest in the development; my salary was barely enough to pay our expenses each month. I used to care about not getting ahead fast enough. Some of my engineering peers from Rutgers were now partners in big consulting firms and vice presidents at banks on Wall Street. Here I was, playing the role of Project Manager in a no-name company in New Jersey, but who cared? Being a good provider for my family was more important than career success.

Then, my heart skipped a beat as I remembered the mess that had been created on the SRD Project. Could it land me on the list of people to lose their jobs? What if we lost the house because I couldn't turn things around? I once again imagined a conversation with my parents about moving in with them until we could get back on our feet. *Simply awful.* My strength was being a good provider. Without that...

Shaking my head quietly, I thought, *Gotta put an end to mistakes like this before I produce a real doozy.*

I had to handle the messages in my inbox immediately. I needed to make sure that things weren't as bad as they seemed.

That guy at the airport had probably gotten through all of his email already, between the curb and the ride home. His family was probably happy to get his full attention at this very moment.

As I paid for my limo, I made my decision. It was time to get a smartphone. It would help stop the errors and I'd have access to email whenever I wanted. Maybe I'd get a BrainPhone like everyone else at work, but I needed the absolute newest and best one.

Lugging my stuff to the front door, I quietly let myself in. This was our usual ritual. I'd try to sneak in to surprise everyone and they'd try to catch me before I got too far. As I clicked the door shut and stepped into the dark foyer, my daughter Lizzy came running, full of squeals, hugs and kisses. Her freckles were just starting to disappear; she looked less like a ten-year-old and more like a teenager every day. Every time I was away from her, she seemed to get just a little bit bigger and older.

Sandy stretched out her arms to surround me in a big, long hug; she squeezed me hard, but I barely noticed: My attention was already in cyberspace, answering SRD emails and finding a BrainPhone store online. Google search terms were already lining themselves up...

My cyber-dreaming stopped when she took my head in her hands and looked me in the eyes. "Bill, Honey...." She was wearing her favorite New York Yankees cap over her dark hair, a T-shirt, jeans and sneakers. Lizzy didn't actually play soccer, but Sandy relished the role of "soccer Mom" and didn't miss her career as a student counselor for even a minute. On most of my first nights back from a business trip, I'd hold her for just a few extra minutes until one of us initiated a game of "How is every little thing?" We'd repeat the question back and forth for a few minutes until one of us ran out of answers. It was our way of checking in after not seeing each other for a long time.

This time, she remembered, but I simply forgot. Sandy quickly asked "Is everything okay? Even every little thing?" She still had the kindest eyes I had ever seen, as they looked quietly into mine, filled with a question I didn't want to answer.

"Yeah, just tired from the trip," I sighed as I kissed six-month-old Rebecca. The truth was that I couldn't wait to put Lizzy to bed and get everything off my mind. Half an hour later, after both kids fell asleep and Sandy started washing up my plates, I slunk upstairs to my home office to start sorting through my email.

First, I searched for a profile for Stevnellie9612@aol.com, but the account had been completely deactivated. There was nothing else I could do to find out who the mysterious sender was.

Fortunately for me, Martha's SRD email was a non-issue. Someone else on the team had corrected her errant message, and we had moved on. I took note of the fact that if I'd had a smartphone, her original email wouldn't have fazed me. All that worrying about making her look feckless wouldn't have happened.

Within the hour, an order for the newest-model BrainPhone was whizzing through cyberspace from a warehouse somewhere in the world, courtesy of eBay, FedEx, and the other gods of online shopping. Once I ordered it, I was amazed at the way the all-knowing Google immediately started flashing banner ads featuring the BrainPhone on every page. One promised "A 50% boost in Productivity. Right Now," and I felt comforted, even though I couldn't shake a nagging thought: *what if this tactic was no better than any of the "Two Thousand and Two Tips in Time Management? What if it failed to get the job done? What then?*

Later that night, as I lay in bed with Sandy, she asked "How did the trip go? Whom did you meet? What did you say? Then what did they say?" These were all the details that she liked to hear, and I normally hated discussing them. Tonight, however, it felt comforting and took my mind off my big dilemma. I didn't want her to worry at all about my situation at work, so I answered the fresh urgency of her questions with quiet accuracy.

I felt better until she told me about the Hernandezes and what was happening to them in Florida.

They were our neighbors and friends -- Rafael and Tonia. Both our families had moved into the Pembroke Lions development in Miramar, near Fort Lauderdale, ten years ago. Luckily, our family returned to New Jersey before the recession started. Dad's first transient ischemic attack made that a no-brainer. From a few thousand miles away, we watched as South Florida suffered some of the worst depreciation in real estate values in the country. Unfortunately, the Hernandezes' home quickly lost about 40% of its value, and their mortgage payments ballooned by over $500 per month. The real disaster struck when Tonia got pregnant and was ordered to leave her job and take full bed rest, just before Rafael's construction company started losing a lot of money. This last fact was new to me, but it made sense.

"He's looking for painting jobs now and the bank is about to foreclose their property. The job market has fallen apart. They sounded awful; Tonia was crying, and poor Rafael couldn't even talk to me. I hope this thing ends soon. Thank God we moved from Florida before all this happened and we aren't in any trouble."

I couldn't talk. My pulse was hammering in my head and I pretended to be half-asleep, afraid that she'd hear my voice shake in the dark. In a bid to end the conversation, I muttered something incomprehensible and tired sounding.

"Even though we moved here to take care of your parents, it was a smart decision. By the way, your Dad wants to talk to you. He wants to get some test done that's not covered by insurance, so he needs to borrow some more money. Thank goodness we are stable and you have a reliable job -- the poor Hernandezes. Thanks for taking care of us, Honey."

She often said this, especially when she talked about how much it meant to our kids to have a stay-at-home Mom. A few minutes later, Sandy was asleep. My body wouldn't cooperate and I stayed wide awake. A cold fear surged through my muscles, which were as tense as piano wires. It was my first sleepless night courtesy of Syscon's layoff list.

* * *

I looked at the clock after what seemed like an eternity – only 2:30 a.m. Lying in bed, I tried to think of what I would do if my smartphone gambit didn't work.

At around 5:00 a.m. I rose to get a cup of coffee then flicked on my laptop. I wanted to get ahead of the day by working off some of the email backlog.

Great. Now I had only 490 email messages.

I started going through them, but by 6:45, I was still groggy. It was time to get to the office, and the email count was now at 455. While I worked, 12 new ones had arrived.

*What was I supposed to do?* I thought angrily, *I'm not some slave to everyone's email!*

Sandy called out, "Time to get to work, Honey," so I reluctantly got up to take a shower, still feeling upset. *I may never catch up.... and what the hell does it mean if I don't?* The thought kept running through my mind as my body went through the motions of getting ready.

Before I knew it, I was pulling up into Syscon's parking lot in Holmdel, a town in south-central New Jersey. Nothing had registered that morning. Sandy, Lizzy, Rebecca, breakfast, the drive to the office. Just as I pulled up the emergency brake in my Saturn, my cell phone rang.

Sandy asked, "Is everything okay? You seemed a bit preoccupied this morning." The concern in her voice was hard for me to hear. I hated the thought of her worrying, and I hated my job for making me feel this way. Biting my lip, I remembered a promise made during much more difficult times: *to never allow my precious wife to slip back into depression.*

"No, darling, it's just that I was looking ahead at what I'd have to do catch up." I stopped and listened, hoping that her concerns would go away.

"Okay," she said, "but remember that you can always talk to me about anything." As an afterthought, she added "You should read this book I'm reading -- it's about how to be inspired by making a difference in the world and how we don't need to be a King or a Lincoln to do great things." She was so utterly sincere and innocent that in the couple of seconds before I could catch myself, my eyes began to flood with tears.

A forced chuckle came from somewhere, sounding hollow and empty. "Nothing to worry about, Honey... but I have to go, as I'm still in the parking lot; plus, I bet Lizzy is asking for her crunchy Cheerios right about now." She laughed back, and her concern seemed to go away. That was good enough for me, for now, so I quickly ended the call and stepped into the parking lot.

\* \* \*

Most people had never heard of Syscon and had no idea what happened behind its whitewashed walls.

To the average outsider, our techie work sounded pretty boring, but I loved it. In fact, I enjoyed it so much that Syscon was the only place I'd wanted to work when I returned from Florida. This was my second stint with the company. The first lasted from 1994 to 2000 and ended when Sandy and I left to live in Florida.

After we moved back to New Jersey in 2005, I was happy to get an offer to return. While working for an insurance company in Florida, I missed the sense of being on a grand quest to educate the world, which was close to Syscon's mission statement.

In spite of all those warm feelings, the last few months had been difficult. Doing the job of three people was hard: I didn't have the time to think freely and come up with new ideas, which I used to treasure. Also, instead of being an industry leader, the company was stuck in competitors' tracks, which made me feel wary. It was a far cry from where we used to be, defining and dominating the computer-based learning industry without much effort.

As I looked up at the building, I felt a pang of disappointment. Syscon's exterior needed a fresh coat of paint, but the building's design still looked quite modern. It was built just before I joined the company the first time, a few years before the Dotcom boom. Upon close inspection, it was obvious that the building wasn't properly maintained. Our senior management just hadn't kept the place up. Broken panes, cracked walkways and missing fixtures would make a keen observer take a second look. A line item budgeted on a spreadsheet had obviously been cut, and it was showing.

The place looked like a dump; it reflected the company owners' state of mind. They were now squeezing 1,000 people into a space designed for 500. A big part of the building was leased to other tenants.

Simply, it was difficult to get excited about doing three jobs each day with no end in sight. According to Ted, my closest colleague at work, "Nowadays, it's all brute force and ignorance." Instead of executing a fine painting like a Renaissance artist, I felt like an ordinary painter from New Jersey who just got the job done using sheer force of will.

As I climbed the stairs to enter the building, I thought about the two goals I needed to accomplish: first, I had to get Martha to approve the purchase of the new BrainPhone that was already being shipped to me via UPS. Given the number of smartphones being carried around Syscon, that wouldn't be too hard.

The second was to show her that I was making a solid attempt to distance myself from the list of those "Most Likely to be Voted Out of the Company." Way too much time watching "Survivor", I thought wryly.

After rehearsing my arguments, I was ready. After all, I'd be using the BP for work and $350 was almost too much for me to handle on my own, considering Lizzy's overdue need for braces. Martha should be willing, I told myself, especially if it would benefit her and Syscon.

As I practiced making my case, I crossed the expensive, Italian marble floors that would never have been installed in these recessionary times. They were still shiny, and the glass atrium let in an abundance of light, lifting the spirits even on cold wintry days. My office was on the third floor, not quite overlooking the sunniest part of the atrium, but near enough to benefit from the generosity of light. I sometimes wondered how office layout affected employee productivity, because the tone shifted markedly once I turned the corner from the corridor into my cubicle farm. I shared a space with 30 people, all squeezed between short walls that rose just above waist height.

My hutch was on the other side of the room, so I had to pass through the crowd to get to its safety. It wasn't so bad this early in the morning, but by 10:00 a.m. the place would look like an ants' nest and sound like a disco. I remembered the scenes from the old movie, "Saturday Night Fever," when John Travolta entered the dance club and had to say hello to everyone, just because they were there and because there were so many of them. By the time I got to my chair, I was exhausted. Being away from the daily routine for a few days always had this effect.

Dropping my briefcase on the floor, I tried not to notice the six-inch stack of papers sitting on my chair or the flashing light on my telephone, telling me that I had voicemail waiting. Instead, I made my way right over to Martha's office. "This should be easy," I imagined. In fact, in the good old days, I would have just picked up the device from the stockroom.

As I caught sight of her silhouette through the frosted glass panel that framed her door, I immediately felt that familiar pull of affection. Right after I had entered the company as a young pup, she had taken me in hand and transformed me from a green college graduate who thought he knew everything into a working professional with a more open mind. She never stopped looking out for my best interests, standing in my corner even when I failed and made her look bad. I trusted her.

Martha took a moment to look up after she heard me rap on her door. Lately, she had taken to wearing reading glasses all the time, which made her look much older than her 55 years. Some gray wisps peeked through her brown, highlighted hair.

She looked alert, but a little frazzled for a Monday morning. "Tough weekend?" I asked as she smiled and welcomed me in. "Not quite, but I'm glad you're back. How was the trip?"

I sat down and told her all about my travel through three airports, the email outage, and the death of my battery. She listened closely with a nod and a laugh as I hyped up the difficult moments. I also gave her a short update on my end of the DAPE project.

"Well, you didn't miss anything too exciting while you were gone," she admitted before updating me on my other projects and the meetings that I had missed.

"Thanks for doing that," I offered, even though it was standard practice.

"Will you be at the department meeting today?"

With a groan of sudden realization, I asked, "Do I really have to go to that? I desperately need to catch up, and I bet I'm getting messages asking why I hadn't responded to earlier messages."

"Just show your face for an hour, maybe before lunch, so you can see and be seen." We both laughed; this running gag had started the day I joined Syscon. Martha had been forced to repeat a ridiculous company policy about "networking" that we boiled down to nothing more than, "See and Be Seen." Any time we wanted to make fun of a showboating colleague, we'd laugh and say "See and Be Seen", sometimes in the middle of meetings, just for amusement.

"Great, now I can really get some work done. I almost stayed home to work through all my email in peace and quiet. But I do want to ask you something. I was wondering... I wouldn't have fallen behind on my email this week if I had had a BrainPhone. Would Syscon pay for me to get one?" I didn't mention that it was already on its way.

She paused for a moment and stood up to close her door. "Actually, that's a good idea, but I want to give you some feedback that you need to hear. It's not all pretty, unfortunately."

# Chapter 2

"Last week, I suggested your name to lead a new project that's coming on stream. It's pretty exciting, and it involves the Zebon technology that you know so much about."

My eyes opened with interest. Zebon was my baby. An open-source technology, it enabled a brand new way to weave in gaming applications with online learning; something I had taken the time to become knowledgeable about it when no-one in the office seemed interested. An opportunity to apply my hard won knowledge would be great. Now, it seemed as if the company was finally going to take it seriously.

"I thought that you'd be just the right person to lead the project, but I got a shock, because none of the other managers in the department agreed. Roger, Matt, Donna, and even Manuel said that they weren't sure if you had the bandwidth. That's the exact word they used.... 'bandwidth'."

Roger and Matt were managers in our department, and Manuel was Martha's boss. Donna was a manager in a different division altogether.

I think my face must have matched the color of her whiteboard, because Martha looked at me carefully before she spoke.

"It's not that you aren't a great guy and that we don't like you; there's nothing personal in this. At the same time, they said that you were making lots of mistakes, plus the tasks you were supposed to do on the NumT project just weren't done at all."

I felt my face getting hot. No one had said a word about the NumT project in months. It seemed to have fallen off everyone's radar, not just my own. As my stomach tightened into a hard knot, I searched for something to say to defend myself. Martha was quietly looking at me, so I just couldn't let it drop.

After an awkward silence, I stammered out, "Is there something specific that they mentioned I should do differently?"

"Well, not really. We talked about this for a few minutes, actually, because you're not the only person who could benefit from some improvements in personal productivity. The problem is that we didn't seem to have a clue as to where we should start. A few of them mentioned Vernon Vaz, the new manager in our division. Have you met him?"

I smiled and nodded. Back in 2005, when I had first moved back to New Jersey, Vernon and I spent a year running together at the Brunswick Running Club. He had just joined Syscon, but over the years we never actually worked together. In fact, we spent more time together on ten-mile treks each Saturday morning than we did at work. We were always part of a large group, and I remember being impressed by how much he knew about running, a sport for which his six and a half foot, lanky frame was ideal. He was a competitive guy who did as much racing as he could and talked often about winning or why he didn't win.

My five feet and eight inches of stocky muscle were more useful for lifting weights, so I drifted to the gym after getting a few running injuries. Over the years, we saw each other in passing in the hallways and remained friendly. I remembered an email message from a week earlier, announcing that he had joined our division.

"I actually know him from outside work -- from the running club in Brunswick." I said so tentatively, because I couldn't see where this was going.

She looked a bit surprised. "Oh really? We talked about him and how well he had been doing. While there've been a few complaints, he's led several projects successfully. Manuel suggested that you find out what he's doing to pick up some of his techniques. Maybe, if you do that, you could learn some stuff that would allow you to take on bigger things. That would be a good thing for Syscon and a good thing for you."

Complaints? A faint memory stirred inside me, as if I had filed some factoid away a long time ago and couldn't quite retrieve it. "What complaints did you hear?"

"Well, I heard that he can be a bit intense."

"That's not bad... I like intense!" I quipped, as Martha smiled in response.

"I hear that they even call him 'Vermin!'" she whispered, as if the room were bugged. We both broke into laughter like a couple of kids.

Now I remembered. I had overheard the name being passed around the office, but my distaste for office gossip meant that I had never made the link between Vernon and his nickname. His style seemed to upset some people.

Our laughter felt good and reminded me of how lucky I was to have Martha as a boss. When we came back to our senses, I asked, "When do I report for duty?"

She adopted a mock-serious face and tone of voice. "I'm not saying go work for him or anything like that. But you might want to stick close to him."

"Okay, is this something I need to do urgently?" I was fishing, because I wanted to know if there was more to this than she told me.

Her voice dropped and she said quietly, "You do know that there are some more cuts coming?"

The world seemed to stop as I found a hitch in my breath. My eyes flickered with fear.

She stopped there, as if she had more to say but couldn't. A heavy silence hung in the air as I looked at her and waited, but her eyes looked down at the floor and she sighed.

"Remember that comment someone made in the last all-staff meeting? That we have too many Project Managers? Just enough Managers and Directors, but too many people at your level. You don't want to be seen as the Project Manager who is stuck at below average performance, do you?"

My mind spun, partly because I thought I always lost the game of "how I was seen" by others. But I also didn't want to be stuck. It stung to realize that she must have agreed with the others' assessment.

"I know -- that's why I'm getting a BrainPhone," I protested. "I'm thinking that it will move me up a notch and if nothing else, I should be able to become way more responsive and stay on top of email."

She added, "Don't get me wrong, that's a great start. But whatever you do, don't do it quietly. The point is to be seen making an effort and to make some actual changes. That's what will shift perceptions more than anything else."

Awkwardly, I added, "And what about Syscon paying for it?"

"No problem with that," she nodded. "Whatever you do, just don't go crazy with that thing. A friend of mine almost lost his girlfriend when...." At that moment, the phone rang, and she answered it.

Her new tone of voice told me that our conversation was over, and I left her office. She shot me a friendly wave and an I'm-sorry-but-I-have-to-get-this look. I wanted more from her, but walked away without trying.

\* \* \*

Back at my desk, I started going through my email. I intended to get through them all before joining the staff meeting. Midway into the third message, I found my mind drifting back to the conversation with Martha.

Leaning back in my chair, I ran through the conversation in my mind, looking for clues that might help me decide what to do next. I hurriedly scribbled down some of the points she'd made.

*Being seen.* Did that mean political game playing on another level? Could I even do that well? Was this even a game? Keeping this job meant that Sandy got to stay home and give our kids her time and attention. It paid our bills and our ballooning mortgage. My parents never had to worry about paying Dad's medical bills. We took the occasional vacation. Disney World at some point. New tires on the car. Braces. I frowned.

Back in the day, only poor performers lost their jobs. Now, wrong place, wrong time and bad luck made that decision. My luck needed to turn around so that I was nowhere near that list.

The company always needed Project Managers, which used to mean that the job was a secure one. Now, with fewer projects, something had to give. Some *people* had to give. The ones on the list.

I pulled up the mystery email from Stevnellie9612@aol.com and read it slowly. Manuel would never show me something like this, but someone had taken the time and the risk to share some insider information. Was it because they cared about me that much? Was it Martha?

No, the tone was all wrong. It wasn't her: the mystery sender didn't feel friendly or helpful. It was more of a warning. But why warn me?

Behind me, I heard chatter and closed down the message. Had to be careful in these damned cubicles - anyone could appear in your space without a moment's notice. A few seconds passed, then I felt a rap on my shoulder.

I whirled around to see Vernon's lanky frame looming over me. He was standing just a little bit too close, making me lean back. I smiled, "Hi Vernon! Welcome to the division." In a twinkle, my mind flashed to fond memories of Saturday morning runs around Edison, Piscataway and Metuchen.

He half-smiled but didn't say anything, leaving an awkward silence that I filled. "How are things on the road... with the club?"

At this question, he nodded but still didn't say anything. This was weird. Was he OK? This wasn't the chatty persona I remembered from those ten-mile runs. Back then, he knew more than anyone else and had fun answering all sorts of questions for less experienced people.

"I hear you are the guy who knows all about Zebon?" It sounded like an accusation.

I gave a puzzled nod and waited. He flashed a forced smile and drew up a chair from nearby." I'd like to learn as much as I can. Both Martha and Manuel said that you were the right person to come talk to."

I settled back in my chair as the tension caused by his clumsy approach slipped away. He sat down and leaned forward, only a few inches away. A bit too close, again.

For the next half hour, I delved into Zebon's intricacies, giving him the essence of what I had learned over the past few years. It was fun telling anyone who would listen about how the principles of gamification could be used by the platform to deepen both the designer and end-user experiences.

Vernon took copious notes while carefully writing down the URLs I recommended. He was an avid BrainPhone user and interrupted our conversation several times to take a call or check email when it buzzed or beeped. He was far away from his desk, but he could still get work done. I badly wanted to do that also, in order to show everyone how effective I could be.

As if he had read my mind, he told me as much. "By the way, you need to get a BrainPhone. Believe me, it's a must for high productivity. These babies are a whole new ball game compared to those old cell phones." He pointed at the five year old basic device sitting on my desk.

Before I could tell him that mine was in the mail, the conversation ended as it had with Martha. He got a call and walked away after giving me that "important call" look. I was left alone staring at his empty seat.

Then it struck me. Why did he want to know so much about Zebon? What was he going to do with what I told him?

"He's a good guy," I told myself, recalling our Saturday morning runs. Still, I felt strangely used, as if my brain had just been picked clean. That feeling passed as I formed a mental picture of my new BrainPhone. I'd use it to show Martha and the others how I could stay on top of things including email.

This would be my ticket to stay off the list. *It had to work.*

* * *

My new BrainPhone took another week to arrive. While it seemed to take an eternity, I couldn't help but notice that Sandy wasn't excited at all. In fact, she showed me every article and YouTube video she could find about the horrors of smartphone use. She showed me stories about crazy people who used them while running in the streets of cities, during church services and in the middle of movies. It was hilarious.

While we were walking in the mall one evening, she pointed out a poor wife trying to communicate with her husband as he tapped away at his keyboard, oblivious to the world around him.

"I hope that's not what you're planning to do, is it?" she asked quizzically, with a hint of sarcasm in her voice. My smile didn't seem to convince her that I'd be any different. There was no way that would happen to me.

Sandy's cousin, Danielle, came to visit for a day. She hardly looked up from her smartphone even once. We couldn't tell whether it was her job, or her friends, or her fiancé, but Sandy and I just looked at each other while shaking our heads quietly. "How rude!" she mouthed to me. "No clue!"

When she left, Sandy made a beeline for me. "Make sure that you don't end up like her."

Shaking my head in disbelief, I replied, "Heck, no."

"By the way," she added, "another letter came from the bank. Up goes our interest rate, once again." She announced this piece of news with a scared tremor in her voice. "I can't wait to get them off our back." She ranted for another minute or two until I interrupted. "Don't worry. We'll get that new mortgage. No matter what." Saying those words made me feel stronger. Sort of.

The following day, my new BrainPhone arrived.

The brown box deposited at the door gave me a little flutter of excitement. The UPS guy had no idea what he had just done for me. Sitting down without removing my jacket, I opened the box with a sharp letter opener. Sandy watched, bemused. She still wasn't thrilled, and I stopped trying to change her mind. If she knew what was really at stake, she'd understand. And there was no way I was going to tell her. Images of dark curtains fluttered into my mind, but I pushed them away to focus on tearing off the wrapping.

Ignoring the instructions, I booted it up. It didn't take long to access my email and surf a few pages. I could feel that things were going to be different now that I could work from anywhere, whenever I wanted.

Over the next few days, I quickly mastered the device. It was well-designed and easy to use; this caught me by surprise. It made the job of manipulating email so much easier than sitting down at my laptop. Each day, I could dip into my email Inbox as many times as I wanted to deal with the most urgent matters. Now, for a change, I weighed in on team concerns from the onset rather than discovering that a decision had already been made.

When Martha and my other colleagues discovered that I now had a BrainPhone, they added me to their instant messenger lists. The BPM system, I learned, was the platform for a tiny ecosystem in the office. As I shared my PIN with them, they mentioned how much they used it "to BPM each other." Facebook, LinkedIn and Twitter were all a few touches away, so within days, I fell in love with the number of people I could now communicate with at odd moments.

I returned email much more quickly and received some nice comments. It looked like something good was happening.

Two weeks after I received my device, I sat down at the dinner table with Sandy, the kids and her friend Mrs. Bainbridge. She was an older, pretentious woman who belonged to Sandy's bridge club as well as a number of influential volunteer organizations. One of them, the Circle C, ran an after-school computer learning program that Sandy badly wanted Lizzy to join. Getting Lizzy into the right activities was one of Sandy's priorities, and she would do whatever she needed to do. Tonight, that included inviting Mrs. Bainbridge to dinner, with her pseudo-Anglo accent and sharp, needling comments.

Sandy made a beautiful seafood lasagna for the occasion. Her Italian grandmother possessed legendary culinary skills, but this was her first time trying her own hand at a recipe handed down by her grandmother. It had taken her all week to find the right ingredients, including the hard-to-find seafood that would make it something special.

As we sat down at the table, however, I felt a bit haunted. At about 4 o'clock, Martha sent me a heads-up email. Apparently, I had forgotten to include some key specs in a document for the DAPE project. I thought I had been diligent in tracking my email, but here, again, something fell through the cracks. The issue was just making its way through the team via email, leading to a grand game of email tag that was in full force among the ten people involved. Unfortunately for us, we were being watched via CC by at least another 20, including two vice-presidents. Lovely.

Some of it must have shown on my face, as Sandy asked me quietly "Is everything okay?"

"Everything's fine," I said, forcing a smile.

Sandy sat down with a nervous smile - I could tell she wanted this to go well. But part of my attention was on my BrainPhone's beep, which would tell me when a new piece of email arrived in my Inbox. Just as we were passing the lasagna, I heard an unfamiliar beep. I discreetly glanced at the screen and saw that I was getting an instant message. Strange. I didn't get too many of those.

It was Martha.

Martha > Sorry to interrupt, got a minute?

Bill > OK

Martha > Manuel heard that specs were missing from that document and now he's on my butt to get it fixed as soon as possible. Can u come into the office early tom morn/Sat?

Now my heart was racing and my hands started shaking. I had to really concentrate on holding the device so that I could read it. I could hear Sandy and Mrs. Bainbridge chatting away, as I started tapping away, with the smartphone below the table.

Bill > OK, what time would work?

I paused, waiting for her reply, when I heard my name "...Bill" at the end of a sentence, filled with a questioning tone that made me look up.

The voice belonged to Mrs. Bainbridge. Sandy and the kids were looking at me intently. Everyone was waiting for me to respond, but I was silent. I had no idea what the question was.

I looked sheepishly at her and tried to laugh it off by saying, "The office is all over me!"

She icily repeated the question about the job market in Florida and the likely prospects for her son, who was moving there. I brushed her off with a short, dismissive answer, eager to get back to BP instant message. By the time I did, Martha had signed out.

I stared at the screen, wondering what to do next. I shot off a short email telling her I'd check my calendar.

When I looked up, Sandy was on the verge of angry tears, which fortunately, neither Mrs. Bainbridge nor the kids noticed. But I knew. And so did she.

* * *

Two hours later, when I crept into a cold bed, my shiny new device felt like a piece of lead. Finding oneself a mere one or two steps away from a lonely night on the sofa can make a man re-evaluate a few things.

What the heck was happening? In spite of her friendly warnings, I had done something crazy. Now I lay in bed with an angry wife who had "nothing to say," feeling guilty that I almost ruined her evening while bringing her to the verge of tears. *You idiot. You didn't almost ruin her evening. Tell the truth. You did.*

But what alternatives did I have? I needed to stay in the middle of things if I hoped to stay off the list. There was no way to go back to the old-style cell phone. People at work loved the fact that I was now a part of the tribe and my PIN was being passed out to people I didn't even like talking to in real life. This BPM world was new to me. Martha, Manuel and all the other managers were included in it, and I was just starting to join conversations that I never even knew existed. Before, they were happily getting stuff done without me. I had been in deeper trouble than I ever knew.

Three days later, the ice thawed and Sandy started talking to me again, but only after I promised never to bring the BrainPhone near the dinner table ever again. Or to breakfast or lunch for that matter. Anything involving food. Or the four of us getting together to interact as a family.

She made it quite clear that this was just the beginning. She pressed me, "Why do you have to do a stupid thing that everyone else does? Doesn't that make you even more stupid, because you know better?"

*Ouch.* I felt the sharp prick of her counseling skills. Do I stay quiet and be thought an idiot, or say something and confirm it? The dilemma left my tongue thick, dry and useless. "Why is it so important to be a part of a stupid club? You'll still have your job as long as you do that well; you don't need to join in foolish behavior, right?"

"Look, Honey, it's just the way things are."

Dr. Roma, Sandy's psychiatrist in Florida was clear. To prevent her from ever having a relapse, stay away from bad news that didn't have a ready solution. Or something like that. Since 2003, Roma's marching orders had been my drum beat. It was advice that I wasn't exactly eager to test in a real life experiment. Better to third rail it and keep moving on, even if it led to tension.

Fortunately, she backed off and let my last, resigned comment end the conversation. Maybe Roma had told her the same thing, and she knew what I was trying to do? *God, I hope not.*

Over the next few weeks, some good did come out of my BrainPhone. Email wasn't getting lost in my Inbox the way it used to, and I still tried to reply as soon as I could, subject to our family's meal times. As far as the game of replying to email, just picture Andre Agassi and the way he used to return a Pete Sampras serve. That was me.

When I learned that the average person checks email more than 20 times per day, it made me stop to think. I easily beat that on a regular day. It was impossible to be the Agassi of email without checking every few minutes. How else would everyone know that I was on top of things?

As my return-of-email skills improved, I started anticipating important email. I could be anywhere, sometimes driving in my car on I-287, when I'd remember that I was supposed to get an update on the DAPE project. In my mind, I'd paint a picture of the message, then glance at my phone for a buzz, beep or flash. When no evidence appeared, I'd check anyway. It's a good thing I did, as the BrainPhone on AT&T sometimes suffered a notification glitch.

People around me in the division began to realize that I was always on and willing to engage. A few whom I didn't know all that well started to come to me for answers in a hurry. The more this happened, the more distance I put between my name and the layoff list. Or so I thought. *There's no way they can let go of the guy who has all the answers.* With every fast response, my safety increased.

There was some hard evidence, too, that I was improving. My Tzinbox score moved in the right direction so that I was hovering near 0. That was cool. Martha had better be paying attention and not just deleting those weekly reports.

These positive indicators made me feel comfortable resuming my Zebon research. No one was paying attention to how much and how quickly kids who played video games learned. Schools were still using books and a few eBooks, but the most efficient education wasn't happening in the classroom.

Lizzy was now taking on Sweet Mary II and III, after knocking off the 25 levels of Sweet Mary I in a matter of days. When I tried to do the same and took a full week to get past the second level, I realized exactly what she had done. Her constant begging for the additional games reinforced the philosophy behind Zebon: the right mix of gaming and learning is powerfully attractive to the human mind.

Syscon's products never explicitly included gaming elements, and Zebon offered a mix of a Learning Management System and Flash interactivity that could turn any educational experience into an adventure. As an open-source platform, any company or individual could use it, and I wanted Syscon to be the first.

Unfortunately for Lizzy, when my BP was banned from all Crossley meals, she also suffered, because the ban included all electronic devices, including her Wii U. However, on the rare occasions when Sandy wasn't around, we took little holidays. Lizzy didn't seem to mind if I checked a message here and there while she played a game or two. As long as I served macaroni and cheese, her favorite, she was happy.

* * *

They say that when you buy a new car, it's amazing to discover how many other people have the exact same vehicle, even in the same color. It's as if they were just waiting until you completed your purchase to bring them out of hiding. So it was with my shiny new BrainPhone, which impressed a few people in the first few days of its unveiling in the office. After a month, everyone appeared to own one.

That included my friend Ted, a fellow engineer who had started working on the same day that I did at Syscon, back in the summer of 1994. He looked almost the same, and still boasted a shock of blonde hair that had only recently started to thin. An avid tennis player, he stayed trim by heading to the courts at least twice a week, telling me that he looked forward to the day when his two young sons were old enough to "give him a good game."

He was a funny guy with a warped sense of cynical humor and an outsized commitment to the little guy that came out in angry rants that only made me laugh. Unfortunately, this didn't make him a favorite in management circles, especially when he made truthful statements like "I have never worked on a project that ended successfully." They saw him as a very smart screw-up.

We were sitting in the lunch room a month after I received my BrainPhone, talking about the growing smartphone insanity. I shared my "Mrs. Bainbridge incident," which solicited a derisive laugh from him and not a drop of sympathy.

"Sue-Ann has been putting me in the doghouse for rampant BP use for years! Welcome to the club. As long as you work around here, there's no escape from our crazy attempts to become more productive." He was shaking his head and looked like a man who had been chastened. Often. To no avail.

"Yesterday, I was in the bathroom, at the urinal you know, with some guy I recognize from accounting. He plays on the softball team with us. This dude was using his phone with two hands overhead when I walked in." Ted stood up to demonstrate. "He was peeing wild and free until he heard me enter. It was as if he realized that I was looking, because he tried to stop, hit the return key and zip up at the same time. That's when the fumbling started, and his BrainPhone came this close to falling into a very wet place. This close. He deserved two points for the shot."

I laughed as, in vintage Ted fashion, he held up his fingers to show me the small distance between communication and disaster.

"But haven't you tried it?" I asked in mock horror that got him laughing. "I'll spread the word: don't borrow his smartphone! Use a landline."

Ted added, "I read somewhere that 16% of smartphones were found to have traces of fecal matter on the keys. These smartphones need to be renamed." We both shook our heads and I wrinkled my nose at the thought of the times when I borrowed others' phones.

"How could such a powerful device lead to such stupid behavior?" I asked out aloud. "Are we really better off?" I held up my BrainPhone and stared at it.

Ted interjected, "It's not the device, Dimwit. Technology is never the problem. We sit there in a meeting or wherever and when things start to get slow, our mind drifts off into imagining what messages we might be getting. The problem isn't silicon, plastic, bits and bytes. It's up here." He pointed to his head. "Our smartphone habits have nothing to do with productivity. Try fear, anxiety, greed, ambition. That's what drives the multitasking at the urinal. It's got nothing to do with productivity."

To be honest, I had done my share of toilet-texting, so I knew exactly what he was talking about, but I just hadn't quite thought about it that way.

"I was in a meeting the other day and noticed that while the poor guy was talking, no one was listening. They were all too busy in the freaking BrainPhone prayer position." I looked lost, so he demonstrated by clicking away at his phone in his lap, just below the surface of the table. It looked like he was praying. That's exactly how I must have looked that morning, in a slow meeting, trying to answer a few short emails.

I knew better than to defend myself when Ted was on a roll. But he was making me think. I thought that I was being more productive by doing some of the things we were laughing about, but now that we were talking about it some more, I started to wonder.

Was this really the way to save my job at Syscon? Was this better productivity, or just greater convenience? Or was it something worse: a mindless, stupid addiction?

In a product update session later that afternoon, I found myself getting annoyed. The meeting convener was interrupting her own remarks to check messages, as if it were the most natural thing in the world. Her attention wandered away, and when it returned, she'd pretend as if she was listening. I wanted to strangle her. It made the damn meeting drag on forever.

That evening as I was driving home from work, I was still seething. As I passed the exit for Edison, I glanced over at a house on a hill overlooking the highway. Smoke poured out of it and a crowd stood outside, looking petrified. It made me think of the Yamashitas, our friends who lived somewhere in that neighborhood. I picked up my phone and started looking for their number. As I glanced back at the road, something yellow flashed in front of me. I jammed on the brakes and felt the car's anti-lock braking system stutter into action as it came to a jerky but final stop. With a solid clunk, I tapped the bumper of a loaded minivan paused in the traffic. A couple of young kids in the back row turned around and looked down.

I pulled over, but the other driver hadn't felt a thing and kept going. There was no sign of any damage, but when I drove off, my heart was in my mouth. 20 minutes later, when I exited the highway, my hands were still shaking.

* * *

About a week later, Maria, an I.T. specialist, wrote a general email that went viral inside the company.

===========================
**Maria Williamson**
-------------------------------------------------
From: Maria.Williamson@syscon.com
To: AllStaff@syscon.com
Subject: MOBILE USE WHILE DRIVING CAN KILL

Last week, I lost my 20 year-old cousin, Hortense, in a car crash to a reckless driver.

He was doing something we all do... texting and driving.

When I got to the crash scene I barely recognized her red Honda Civic.
-------------------------------------------------

She went on to beg everyone who read the email to immediately stop the practice. To bolster her plea, she included some statistics: 4.6 of every 6 seconds texting were spent looking at the device rather than the road. Her lobbying had an effect, because HR quickly announced a task force to work on a new set of policies to ban the practice while performing company business.

The new rules were modeled after the guidelines set by the Federal Government, reinforcing my decision to stop. Unfortunately, in the week after the policy was released, I caught myself texting while driving at least four times without even thinking about it. Eventually, I hid my phone in my briefcase before driving off to force myself to pull over if needed. This was the only thing that worked.

After reading HR's announcement, I set Zebon aside for a few hours to research "multitasking." I learned that what most people called multitasking was actually single tasking. The time and attention spent switching between tasks made multitasking less effective in reality. Even those who thought they were good at it turned out to be worse than average when their performance was actually measured.

Simple multitasking, like walking and chewing gum at the same time, was easy for us humans. However, when both tasks required a cognitive load (like watching a football game and listening to the wife's instructions on what to do with the laundry), that was different. Smartphones in every pocket encouraged everyone to pick up habits that actually killed productivity, according to the recent findings. The evidence was unambiguous.

But I didn't want to believe it: I had a job to save. So I closed the browser and opened up a Facebook page on my BrainPhone. I had a few people to poke.

* * *

Just after the new corporate policies that covered texting and driving came out, I attended a breakfast meeting at a nearby Hilton hosted by a company with a strong interest in Zebon. The local firm, called RingCORE, made computer games for several platforms and directed them at older teens and young adults. A number of local engineers were invited to explore new technologies that the company was considering developing. Zebon was just one of about ten different topics to be discussed in small groups on that late Tuesday morning in August.

At the start of the meeting, they passed around a basket to collect all mobile devices. *Unusual, to say the least.* It was standard practice, they explained, so as their invited guest, I complied. At Syscon, we never did that.

To help keep the session on track, they also used forms with blank spaces for the meeting's purpose, agenda, attendees and action items. It all seemed a bit over the top, but the meeting was short and undeniably effective.

Afterwards, a guy from RingCORE named Mike Springer approached me in the hallway. We grabbed a couple of chairs in an empty conference room.

He was a tall, athletic type with long black hair pinned back in a neat ponytail. It should have been flecked with grey, given that he was older than me. He fidgeted with a restless energy as we sat down, then pulled out a list of questions that he had obviously spent a long time to prepare. As he explained the purpose of the meeting, he spoke in a staccato voice that kept me on my toes. This was not going to be a relaxed wind down from the main event.

"I have 43 questions," he announced at the beginning. "How much time do you have?"

With that setup, we delved into his list, which proved to be full of deep, insightful questions. From the very beginning, I felt stretched. He didn't know much about Zebon, but his questions tested my knowledge. The truth was, I couldn't answer any of his tough questions definitively, and all I could give him were a series of updates on the questions he raised.

During our conversation, he revealed an unusual practice. Whenever I reached for my BrainPhone to check my email or send a quick message, he'd stop talking. It was disconcerting, because everyone at Syscon knew that a conversation didn't stop just because the other person started using their BP.

At first it seemed as if he was just thinking things over for a moment; it happened a few times before I realized that he was deliberately shutting up.

When we got to the 21$^{st}$ question, it was time for us to leave. I asked, "You stopped talking whenever I picked up my BrainPhone. That wasn't a coincidence each time, was it?"

He quickly shook his head, "No."

My confused look made him add, "I like to get 100% of someone's time when I talk to them, so when there are interruptions, I don't try to overrule them."

I sat there feeling confused and a bit chastened.

The lame excuse that I offered came from habit, more than anything else. "I can multitask pretty well." The stupid feeling that came over me must have registered with him, because he didn't say a thing for a moment. All that research I did on multitasking was lost in a vain attempt to avoid looking bad.

"We tried doing that longer than you can imagine. It didn't work for us, so we changed our policies to allow for single points of focus wherever we could. For example, we changed the expectation around email; we only check it two or three times day."

This strategy wasn't new to me, but Mike was the first person I had ever met who was working in an environment that was transformed in this way. "What's it like? How does it compare with what you were doing before?"

"Like night and day. We simply don't use email for emergencies, which prevents all of us from having to check it all day. We can focus on doing more important work instead."

As we walked out to our cars, my attention wilted even though I was excited about this different approach to email. The intensity of the morning's meeting was taking its toll. He, on other hand, appeared even more energized and excited, walking with a bounce in his step.

"Let's keep in touch," he suggested. "We want to get this thing right, and you are the one who knows more about it than anyone else I have met."

"I think that I have just been asking more questions about this stuff than anyone else, that's all!"

"Hey... sometimes that's what it takes. I really appreciate the time you have taken to become an expert on Zebon. I want RingCORE to use it to help us get to the next level – we'll be able to offer more than video games."

His blue eyes looked at me with an unnerving intensity that didn't let go until I nodded with understanding. He understood some of what I had gone through to take this from a hobby into a serious business interest. Not even Martha appreciated that.

As I made my way back to my office, I could feel my phone weighing heavily at my hip. Obviously, something bad had happened to my plans to save my job by becoming a hardcore BrainPhone user. Now that I was indeed addicted, I had new problems and none of the solutions I wanted.

I certainly wasn't standing out from anyone in the office. Everyone, including the guys in the mailroom, had BrainPhones. We all had developed bad habits, while some had become addicted. But where were the gains?

It was cool to be able to grab information in unusual places. Family trips to the shopping mall, for example, turned into extended office hours. That was an improvement over schlepping behind Sandy from one fabric and hobby store to another, dying from boredom.

Of course, she might not have agreed. Lizzy certainly wouldn't. She learned to ask questions to grab my attention as soon as I started tapping away at the keyboard.

Did the greater convenience add up to an increase in productivity? It wasn't clear to me as I walked upstairs to my cubicle, deep in thought.

My mood darkened as it began to dawn on me that I may have just run a long fool's errand. A two month waste of time.

Later that afternoon, I stopped by my desk after a meeting and found a bright yellow Post-It note stuck to my computer's screen. "See me when you can -- Martha."

I crossed the hall and poked my head in.

"Hi, Bill," she said and beckoned me to sit with a tired wave of her hand.

"I need to talk with you" she started, with a slow voice that carried a hint of sadness. "You aren't making the kind of progress that I'd like to see with your time management and productivity," she started.

Then she gave a couple of examples that I knew about – a meeting I was late for, a deliverable that I had missed. They weren't surprises. I had been trying hard not to think about them. The problem with these examples was that they had both happened in public ways that Manuel and the managers could see and remember.

I shouldn't have been surprised. My Tzinbox indicators had fallen back to a -6, indicating clearly that I was in trouble. The software had even sent me a text message with a warning, which came as a surprise. The initial effort to empty my Inbox after getting back from Shreveport had worn off, and I was back at 200 messages in my Inbox. As my manager, she also received a Tzinbox report card summarizing my performance.

She continued in her careful, empathetic style. "I want us to try something else, because there's a meeting coming up in a week or two to discuss this layoff, and I want to make sure that you have a solid plan that separates you from the others who might be at risk."

I gulped and asked, strained, "What do you have in mind?"

# Chapter 3

She certainly had something in mind - a complete reorganization of the DAPE project.

"The execs have decided to combine your project with one coming from the new division." My blank look spurred her on. "Your team is going to be dispersed throughout the company into permanent roles, and we're going to assign you to a project being run by Vernon Vaz. We'll continue to call it the DAPE project due to its major point of focus."

"What?" I sounded startled but didn't mean to object. "I'm sorry, that came out wrong. Tell me more."

"Should be good news. He's brought quite a few projects to completion. He has a decent track record. The company sees him as the best project manager around. You should be able to learn some good things from him, so this should benefit your time management and productivity. He's become a bit of a role model in the eyes of the executives, and I think you're smart enough to figure out how to use some of his methods."

"I heard some good things, too, but also a few bad things. 'Incredibly zealous.' That's what one person told me. Did you hear anything about him being a control freak?"

"No, but that wouldn't surprise me. Good project managers often get tagged with that complaint. Look, I wouldn't worry about that. Try to see what he does to be successful, then use the experience to expand your bandwidth."

Her use of the term "bandwidth" made me remember. This was more than a growth opportunity. She was throwing me a lifeline after my smartphone plan failed to deliver the improvements that I'd promised.

"Well, I'm glad for this opportunity. It looks like a great chance. Combined with my newfound ability to use a BrainPhone in meetings and in the john, I should be okay."

She chuckled, and so did I.

"Looks like you're okay with the idea of working for him?"

"I'm kinda looking forward to it, yes." It was not completely true. But close enough.

"Word is, he has some technique that he thinks we should all be using called MTM, or MGM, or something like that. Manuel is all for it and apparently he uses it himself every day. He wants us all to get some training."

"Oh yeah, that's the Master Time Method. I attended an MTM training a long time ago, and I found it helpful. I still use some of it."

"Great -- you can help make us all better. God knows that I could use a dose of some good time management techniques. My mother complains that she never sees me anymore."

"Not to worry. I'll go find the secret sauce and bring it back to our division."

She shook her head in mock frustration.

"Plus, I want to know what he did to earn the nickname 'Vermin'." I didn't say this out loud, but it was on my mind. One or two people had mentioned it, but no one really knew where it came from. The fact that it was out there hung around in my mind like a mosquito I couldn't quite shake. But his nickname wasn't the point.

As I left her office, I reminded myself, "It's the list, stupid. It's all about staying off the list."

* * *

On the way back to my desk, I took a detour to the cafeteria for a cup of tea. Today, I needed my afternoon treat before hitting the road with all the traffic that it promised.

Sitting down by an open window with a fresh cup at hand, I surveyed the empty cafeteria. The clock was announcing the reason no one was around; it was already 5:30 p.m.

Outside, there was a slight drizzle. It was one of those unusual summer days with both sun and rain, and it made me feel both melancholy and hopeful. It was easy to relax into this peculiar mix of feelings as I let the day's happenings soak in.

RingCORE was up to some fascinating stuff. Or maybe it was just Mike? Wherever it came from, it was intriguing. After talking with him, it was obvious that my smartphone plan had created problems for me that they'd already solved. I felt a bit silly. Fixing my time management issues wasn't as easy as buying the latest gadget.

New Technology + Bad Habits = Chaos. I wrote this equation in my notebook. BrainPhone Corporation didn't care about my habits and provided no training in how to use its devices to become more productive. Yet, the BP was powerful enough to shape millions of people's habits in ways that they didn't fully understand or appreciate.

Now, I needed to find a way to unlearn some habits. Where was the gadget to help me do that?

My mind snapped back to "the list."

Perhaps Martha was right; working with Vernon could help me keep my job. It was the only thing I could think of trying, now that new technology wasn't the answer. I was enthusiastic about the Master Time Method training back in 1999, when it was the best thing since sliced bread. Leaving that program, I was in a hot hurry to implement every last detail, even its strange redefinition of words such as "now" and "space."

At the time, I had been 39 years old, married for three years and Sandy was pregnant with Lizzy. It certainly made a big difference by helping us survive the move to Florida a few months later. My MTM book was still somewhere on my shelves, unopened for several years.

Back when I was a member of the running club, Vernon was one of those people who always talked about doing things faster and gave out lots of useful advice. I'd find out next week what he was like on a project team here at Syscon, but maybe I could get things moving in the right direction. Before the announcement went out.

That seemed like a good plan. I sat there for a few more minutes, daydreaming of what it would be like to carve out a new reputation for myself. Perhaps I'd tell him about my predicament and my fear of being placed on the list. He might help me turn things around, and I could end up enjoying the kind of relationship with him that I had with Martha.

It would be great to have some help and not be so alone in all this mess.

My thoughts were interrupted by a beep on my phone announcing a text message. It was Vernon. "We need to talk. Are you in the building?"

The message seemed a bit cryptic and a little cold, in that text-message kind of tone. I replied, "Yes, how about early next week?" I waited a few minutes, but when I didn't get anything back, I finished off my cup before grabbing an elevator to my office. We could figure out when to meet later in the week.

When I got to my cubicle, it was empty except for a single, tall, crew-cut figure talking on a phone near my desk. Vernon.

* * *

I approached conspicuously so that he could see me, but he hardly acknowledged me and kept talking.

As he turned his back to me to continue talking, I settled down at my desk. He was one of the few people at Syscon who still wore a tie every single day, favoring bland designs with crisp, white button-down shirts. He wasn't a military veteran, but "boring tie and white shirt" was his uniform.

"My daughter, Neleta," he said, shaking his head before rolling up a seat.

"How's the running?" I asked, thinking that we could start off a bit informally.

"Good. Let me tell you how we are going to save the DAPE project." Inside, I jumped. *Didn't know it was in trouble.*

He started telling me all about my part of the project, what was wrong with it and where it needed to go. I tried to get a word in here and there, but he ignored my attempts to add information; he just kept going and going like the Energizer Bunny. Most of the background he was "filling me in on" was stuff I already knew intimately. I listened intently, thinking that he'd eventually get to some breaking developments, but after fifteen minutes of repetition, we were right back where we started.

"We need to win," he said. Not just once, but over and over again in different ways. "Show everyone that this is the best project." Then, "Make a name for ourselves," and finally, "Demonstrate superior execution based on our results."

But if we were going to win, who would the losers be? Or was this just about him winning? Rumors around the office said that he was a few steps from being promoted, so that could be what he really meant.

The good part was that he was nothing like other Syscon project managers, who never got gung-ho about anything. I liked his fresh energy. It was infectious, and I felt myself getting caught up in it. He smiled as he created a picture of what this opportunity could mean for all of us and our careers. "This could help define the future, if we just do an extraordinary job."

He leaned in with a tight focus on my eyes, in a stare that was almost hypnotic. I started to believe and nodded in all the right places, which cranked up his intensity. He liked it when I agreed with him. This was the Vernon I remembered from Saturday mornings, who kept on talking even when the rest of us ran out of steam halfway into the run.

When he paused to check email on his smartphone, I realized that I hadn't learned anything new, but I was feeling more hopeful about my future. Duplicating his enthusiasm would be a disaster, but improving my productivity looked simple (and distinctly possible) in that moment. I'd just have to get used to long monologues.

At the 30 minute mark, I was dying to end the conversation as the clock approached 7 p.m. It wouldn't get dark until 9 p.m., but I wanted to spend some Indian summertime with the kids. That was my family's special name for these long afternoons, based on a picture that Lizzy had brought home in the second grade, which was still mounted on the fridge door.

"Bill... The Master Time Method... some call it MTM... have you used it?

"Yeah," I said, answering his question, "I have used it." He had to repeat the question because I missed it the first time due to my in-conversation daydreaming. "Remember, we..." Before I could remind him that we both attended Master Time Method seminars back in 1999, he launched into another monologue.

This time, I didn't lean forward expectantly. Instead, I tried to jump in to tell him that I did understand the principles behind MTM and that we had discussed them at length after one of our runs a few years ago. I didn't make a dent, and fifteen minutes later, I was exhausted. Then he pulled a copy of the Master Time Method book out of his briefcase. He held it up and pointed at it like Vanna White would a featured product.

"Have you ever heard of it?" He asked the question with a tone that suggested, "Of course you haven't." Didn't I just tell him that I'd used it? Wasn't he listening?

I nodded, but before I could reply, he jumped back in. "Then you have got to take a look at it again. It's been a while, right?"

"Why, are you guys using it?" I asked with a straight face.

"Using it?" he exclaimed with enthusiasm. "Does a preacher use the scriptures? It's the only reason I keep bringing projects in on time. Almost everyone who works with me has read it, so here's my copy. Let me know when you're done and we can talk about your implementation. You can help me bring some sanity to this place."

I held my hand up, "That's okay, I have a copy at home."

These words registered and he paused. Finally. Seizing the moment, I picked up my briefcase and started putting stuff in it.

Not a pause. Five minutes later he was quoting lines from the book, going on about the brilliance of Xavier Kripanali. Without waiting for the right moment, I stood up, feeling like a sinner leaving a service midway.

"Wait -- do you wanna come?" I had no idea what he had just said. "To Minneapolis, to attend a Master Time Method workshop with me? It's a three day refresher course."

Now, he was standing, blocking my way to freedom.

*Sure*, I thought, *it's right up there with getting a liver transplant*. What I actually said was "I doubt that I'll be able to find the time." And there was no way that I wanted to spend the money, either, as the company wouldn't pick up the bill. I tried my best not to sound too snarky. After all, Martha had made it clear that I needed to create the impression of better productivity.

Running to Minneapolis didn't qualify as "better productivity." "But I am looking forward to reading the book again" I added hopefully with as sincere a smile as I could muster. Now, I was the one channeling Vanna White. "But look at the time -- it's 7:20, Dude! I have to cut this short, but listen... my copy of MTM at home has all my notes in it."

He stared at me, still standing in my way, when the smile fell away. A short step brought him inches from my face and I squared my shoulders expecting to smell his breath as he drew himself to his full height. His lips pursed as he rasped out his parting shot, "Hope you make it, buddy..."

What did he mean? Make it to what? Did he know something about the list? What was he talking about?

In a quick second, I formed all these questions, but before I could put them together, he took a step back and wheeled away from my cubicle. Picking up my briefcase, I took a baby step that took all the energy I had. I stopped, took a clear, deep breath, and put one foot in front of the other all the way to the door, with my heart thumping.

* * *

When I got home that evening I was still shaken. Obviously, Martha had told him more than I expected. Or maybe he'd just figured it out? Was he on a fishing expedition?

I scowled at the thought of my shocked face when he had muttered, "Hope you make it..." It probably told him more than he knew, but now I had no choice but to wait and see what he would do next. The tone of his comment made me think that things could get a little nasty. Or worse.

Lucky for all of us in the Crossley household, Sandy and the kids were visiting my parents. Giving up on Indian Summertime, I dumped my stuff in the office and found my copy of the Master Time Method on the shelf.

Without bothering to remove my work clothes, I relaxed into my easy chair, pausing only to slip off my shoes. I needed some time to think this over, so I turned on some instrumental reggae.

Was Vernon trying to help me? Did he have a heart of gold, but no interpersonal skills? *God, I hoped so.*

I glanced over at a picture of Sandy, Lizzy and Rebecca playing on the swings in Stelton Road Park, all decked out in Fall colors. The day looked like a happy one, and my heart began to fill. Away from everyone, sitting in the warmth of my home, I started choking up. A thick, heavy sob escaped my chest.

My head shook "No," and a deep, new breath seeped in slowly. The best way for me to take care of them right now was obvious. It didn't involve a pity party.

When they came home three hours later, I was half way through the book. I hadn't budged an inch and barely looked up, even when the kids came in to hug me and Sandy gave me a strange look.

She had brought a corned beef sandwich home for me, which I hardly noticed, even though it was one of my favorites.

"Haven't you read that book already?" she asked when she saw what I was doing.

I'm on a new team at work," I shot back, "and I need to see what they are doing. Plus, it was a long time ago, and the DAPE project at work has been brought under a new division."

I must have been a little strained or even clipped in my tone because she stood for a moment and stared at me. When her face formed the start of a question, I gave her a pained "please don't start with me" look, causing her to sigh. She picked up the wrapper from the sandwich and made her way to the kitchen.

I threw myself back into the book. So far, it was all a historical review, as the memory of what I had learned in the 1999 class came trickling back. It felt like rooting around in an attic looking for something that had been lost years ago. Maybe I had forgotten something useful that could turn things around. This thought filled me with hope and energy, even after a long day.

Although a long time had passed, I noticed that there was a lot in the book I still used and a few things I had discarded. There were other things I had completely forgotten about; reading about them was pretty interesting, but I couldn't find anything earth shattering or groundbreaking. Over the years, I had clearly come up with something better, just by making an odd improvement here and there.

At 11 p.m., I finally got up out of my chair, exhausted and unable to keep my eyes open. The recent meetings with Mike, Martha and Vernon had left me feeling drained. In the aftermath, they felt more like encounters.

At the same time, I was perplexed. What was I supposed to do differently at this point? Anxiety started to creep in as I imagined myself unable to improve my time management skills and getting fired, even after all this effort. Here I was, desperate to find a way out of this predicament; that could only happen if I made a new impression.

I made a decision - I'd ask Vernon what he thought I could do, based on how my own methods for managing myself had evolved over the years. He seemed to have a good understanding of how MTM worked and had probably encountered the same problems himself. Maybe he knew other people who had also customized the system for themselves.

When I finally crawled into bed, I expected to find Sandy half-asleep. As I leaned over to give our usual goodnight kiss, her body tightened.

"Bill, what's going on?" It wasn't a friendly, warm question. Instead, it was filled with fear and stress. My body stiffened. She didn't need to know anything about this. Not now anyway.

My mind flashed back in time. I was eleven when my father's employer was the target of a hostile takeover. He came home from the chemical processing plant in Rahway each day and gave us all the detailed happenings for over two years. At first, I enjoyed listening to the unfolding drama the way kids like to hear adult conversation, but in the final six months, my Mom entered a deep depression. It was an awful experience, and the thing I most remember was the set of curtains in her bedroom, drawn all the time. There were long, dark mornings when she couldn't get out of bed. My poor Mom had suffered, and I couldn't help.

I wasn't going to inflict any of that on Sandy, whose own mother had been severely depressed for years and was forced to take daily medication to function. Back when we lived in Florida, Sandy passed through her own blue period, but, with the help of Dr. Roma, she had bounced back after a few months. That was too damned close for comfort.

Since then, I had used his advice to stay vigilant for early signs. One symptom was called "blunt affect": a flat voice that lacked any trace of life. Another was long periods of silence. I did my best to keep away scary news that could trigger these symptoms, always keeping in mind how much my Mom had suffered. Sandy needed my protection.

Manning up, I tried to sound confident. "Nothing, just work stuff that couldn't wait."

My reply still sounded weak and stupid. I silently prayed that it would do the trick. I just needed some time to fix things.

She took a deep breath and sighed. It didn't sound like relief: more like exasperation mixed with resignation. I left it at that.

My mind turned to planning what time I'd need to get up before work tomorrow so that I could finish reading the book, but before I could doze off, my BP rang. I mumbled a "Hello?"

It was Vernon.

"Hey, Billy, I wondered if you could come in early on Monday. Martha and Manuel asked me to add the Minnesota Team to our project. I need you to come in to get some early instructions."

He paused. So did I, but not because I was having trouble remembering what my calendar looked like. More work?

I heard myself say, "Yeah -- what time?"

"How about 6:30 a.m.?"

I groaned inside and agreed. What choice did I have?

"Have you started on the MTM book yet?"

"Actually, yes, I have."

"It's good, isn't it? Did you notice the way that the parts fit together? It's cool, right? I remember when Xavier produced this cool video that showed quite clearly that..."

I paused, looking at the phone in mock disbelief. His voice was chattering away without a pause; he didn't care if I was listening.

"Vernon, I have to go." Without waiting for an answer, I hung up, too tired to consider the irony that I was supposed to be trying to impress him. Sandy looked over at me and asked, "Who was that?"

I lay back down before answering her. "Just someone from work, don't worry about it."

Apparently, that advice was only for her. My body tossed and turned all night.

# Chapter 4

At 6:30 a.m. sharp, I sat in the conference room all by myself, trying not to yawn. Was I in the right place? Maybe the meeting was actually at 7:30 a.m. and I had made a mistake because of how tired I was.

Couldn't this meeting have been held later?

Vernon burst in a few seconds later with a smile on his face, which fell when he saw me sitting there alone. He looked as if he had lost a game.

"Oh, Bill -- good to see you here." The disappointment filled his voice. "Let's wait to see what time the others get here."

I looked at my watch - 6:34 a.m. *What was he up to?* "I want to make this new DAPE Team an extremely efficient one, and being on time is just the start. We are all going to be using the Master Time Method so that this kind of thing doesn't happen again."

He almost never said "MTM"; he always spelled out the entire name of the approach. Kinda weird.

"The book has some important ideas I want us to use." Once again, he went back to teaching mode, telling me more of the principles from the book. This time, he talked about the importance of meeting commitments and writing them all down. Once again, I had the same thought, "Didn't I just tell him yesterday that I had read the book? Didn't he remember that we once took the same class?"

I didn't want to tell him that I re-read most of it the previous night, because I didn't want to make it look like I was sucking up or desperate. Which I certainly was.

"How will we tackle the fact that we all don't know where DAPE is at the moment?" I jumped in with my question when Vernon paused to look at his watch while shaking his head. As if he didn't hear me, he continued his lecture.

When he paused for a breath, I added, "I actually started reading the book again last night, Vernon," with just a hint of finality in my voice. "You should know what I'm talking about," he continued, trying even harder to put some daylight between his deep knowledge and my seemingly shallow experience.

He did know a lot, but the more he talked, the more uncomfortable I became. Was this about knowledge or control?

"Frankly, just between the two of us, using the Master Time Method is the reason I'm on the verge of being promoted." Astonished at his honesty, I nodded sympathetically, thinking that the conversation was about to come back down to earth.

"Wow, thanks for..." Before I could acknowledge his sharing, he jumped back in, cutting me off in mid-sentence.

"It's why we all have to use it if we want to get ahead. Or even stay in the race." *Was that a knowing look?*

"It would be a good thing if we all could be on the same page with this," I agreed. "If we could all get our days under control, we'd all benefit from having balanced lives. We'd have a shared, calm mind rather than just lots of individual ones."

He looked at me strangely. "Yeah, but the book doesn't say anything about a shared calm mind. Only individual. It's possible only if we use as little memory as possible and instead employ storage tools, like laptops or smartphones. All the stuff we need to do should be placed on a master list and then assigned to the right sub-list. Nothing has changed, or will change, since Xavier wrote the Master Time Method in 1999."

This was straight from the book. But surely it would be easier to accomplish this goal if we were all aligned in some way? I swallowed my concern - why fight over a relatively small point? It was something I could push for later, and besides, I could see a bigger problem looming if I wanted to switch back to MTM.

In the past, I had stopped using multiple task lists and switched over to a single schedule, which was forbidden by the book. It was clearly stated. "Put nothing in your calendar except appointments with other people." What I had done was a very big no-no according to him, and I would suffer from trying to use my schedule in this way.

Vernon, I had hoped, could be convinced that this tweak wouldn't be a problem, but based on what I had just heard, I began to think that he might have a problem with it. That thought made me a little anxious. *Is this the right time to get into this with him?*

Just then, the door opened and the other team members came in, armed with coffee and muffins from Starbucks. They were laughing and chatting when they entered the room.

As they took their seats at around 6:45, I saw that Vernon was smiling and seemed genuinely happy to see them. Apparently, they had already been told that he was going to head up the DAPE Team.

The first part of the meeting went well enough, with a review of DAPE's progress. A couple of hours later, I sensed the meeting coming to a close, but Vernon switched topics.

"I want to address team efficiency first. I have the perfect tool for us to use, so that we can get this project done on time and within budget." He pulled out a new copy of MTM and said, "We're all going to be using the Master Time Method on this project, without exception. That will make the DAPE project the best one you have ever worked on."

There was a dead silence as whatever energy there was in the room before he made this pronouncement was sucked out, as if someone had turned on an industrial-strength shop vacuum.

He didn't seem to care or notice as he continued.

"This is the best approach in the world to personal productivity and time management, so we're all going to use it from now on. Don't worry about the cost, as I'm going to buy us all the books, and anyone who wants to take Xavier Kripanali's class can do so at my expense. I'm confident that you can learn all the techniques that I have used for so many years. You have what it takes."

Now he was looking directly at me as he loomed over the meeting table.

The other members of the team were squirming.

There was an awkward silence after he finished speaking. Everyone looked guilty, as if he was talking about them.

Ted ventured a guess, "Does this have something to do with us coming to the meeting late? There's a good reason for that, you know."

Vernon held up his hand. "I'm sure there is. But I think you'll agree that we are past the point of excuses. Let's move forward to better performance, shall we? Using the Master Time Method will get us to the place where we can be effective team members."

I looked around the room to see bodies shifting uncomfortably. By the time I glanced back at Ted, his face was slightly red and his eyes were blazing.

"Actually, Vernon, I read it several years ago and decided that it wouldn't work for me." His voice was cold and hard.

Vernon smiled and his voice stiffened in an instant transition that caught me by surprise. "I suggest that you go back and read it again. You must have been rushing. This is a requirement for being on the team."

As Ted glanced over at me, I gave my head a small shake, signaling for him to drop it for now. He seemed to think for a moment; then he looked down at the table and sighed. He fell silent.

And he had a point. After that weekend of rereading the book, I felt like I had just studied an extensive rulebook. Kripanali was quite authoritarian, "Do it this way or else." It laid out precise prescriptions that weren't designed to be flexible at all.

To make things worse, like a bad software manufacturer, he claimed repeatedly that the system was "completely error-free." He implied that people who decided to depart from his instructions, as I had, needed to have their heads examined. It also meant that there would never be an MTM 2.0. There would never be a need to develop one.

It meant that I had a problem. Was I still "following" MTM, considering all the changes I had made? Hadn't everyone who read his book or taken his class made their own modifications and adopted commonsense improvements? 1999 was a long time ago. I also noticed for the first time that the book was simply a detailed description of his personal habits. There was no research to back his system up with facts. It had a lot of "follow me" stuff in it. A whole lot.

Vernon didn't see any of it, and instead, he repeated the speech he'd given me earlier about the value of the ideas in the book. As he delivered his mini-sermon for the apparently unconverted, he told us that he wanted to "see our lists" from time to time. Not the personal ones, he assured us, just the ones from work. He wanted to coach us in doing things the right way. For the benefit of the team.

He added, "And I also want to make sure that you aren't using your calendars for anything more than appointments with other people. That's not how the Master Time Method is to be used."

Now, I knew I had a problem. I hadn't kept long lists like that for years. Glancing around, I could see that no one else seemed happy with this piece of news. I was instantly annoyed, and my body stiffened. "Look people, there really is a right way to manage your time, and we are going to be successful because we will do things the right way."

My back started to throb with the tension that I was holding inside. I didn't want to show that I was hating every minute of this nonsense. He didn't seem to be the kind of guy who would leave me alone to do my own thing - not with such an outright challenge to MTM's rules.

The room was silent as we sat, stunned, while he made sure to circle the room and eyeball everyone. Debi was looking down, with her auburn hair hanging around her face. She looked so happy when she'd first come in, but now she wasn't even looking up. He called out "Debi," and when she looked up, he made sure that she also nodded in agreement.

I grabbed the opportunity to glance at my watch in order to announce, "Vernon -- it's time for the department meeting." It was all my team members needed. Like high school students at the sound of a bell, it took them only a few seconds to grab their stuff before rushing out of the room, leaving Vernon and me.

He looked irritated and said out aloud in a nagging, high-pitched voice that seemed directed at himself - "I'll have to do some work to whip these people into shape."

* * *

On my way back to my cubicle, it was impossible to escape the feeling that an awful meeting had just ended, but something much more difficult was just about to start.

Two other meetings that morning whizzed by unnoticed. I'm pretty sure my body was in them, but my mind was stuck in the meeting with Vernon, Ted and the others. 12 to 18 more months of meetings like this would provide Vernon with an endless supply of opportunities to clarify things for the rest of us. *Kill me now. Please.*

Still, it was better to be dead with a job than without. For some reason, that thought held little comfort.

During lunch, some old personal development training I'd picked up in the late 1990's kicked in, and I tried to put myself in Vernon's shoes. What was he going through? What was it like to be held accountable for a project of this size? What if I had only MTM as an option? What would I do?

As corny as it seemed at the moment, it worked a bit. Back in the meeting, when Vernon had shared the deadlines the executives had set for the project, we all groaned in unison. Aggressive? Well, more like "reckless." Or maybe "wishful." He was anxious to meet the targets and announced, "They are a challenge, like trying to run a sub-four hour marathon."

Later that day, Ted stopped by my office.

"He thinks he has us now, doesn't he?" Ted stood at the doorway, shaking his head and smiling wryly.

"What did he say? 'Team efficiency!'" He snorted and shook his head. "Bull! That stuff is nonsense -- he actually thinks that he can ram this crud down our throats and force us to accept it."

I took a deep breath. "Not to defend Vernon here, not in terms of his approach. He's going to make this more difficult than it has to be. But I have been rereading the MTM book, and its principles do make sense."

Ted looked at me as if I was crazy.

"I'm serious here -- there's some value to the method laid out in the book, and it's better than nothing. When I first read it in 1999, it helped me a lot. I started using parts of it back then and never stopped."

"How in the world can it help us? I don't get it."

"There's a benefit to having us all use a good method to manage our time. We would answer our email more efficiently, for example. Look how many messages end up being sent without a reply of any kind. That's one problem that we could fix as a team. It would make a big difference."

Ted shook his head and pursed his lips. "Okay, I'll give you that point... there might be some value there, but who's to say anyone of us can implement something so complicated in such a short time? I tried reading it five years ago and put it down after an hour. Which of us is going to be able to put all that stuff in place, all at once? We're not exactly youngsters. Or magicians."

I nodded. "No easy answer for you there, buddy. It took me a year to adopt many of the practices laid out in the book. Then, I taught myself some practices that weren't in the book, and that took even longer."

"Years? We're talking about weeks! He's not going to allow us the luxury you had."

It was hard to be optimistic. Vernon's my-way-or-the-highway approach was only going to make things more difficult, even though I felt lucky to have a bit of a head start.

Ted's voice got louder. "And, to make things worse, it makes no sense that we all should follow the same method. I'll bet a thousand bucks that each of us don't end up using MTM the same way, if we use it at all."

I nodded in agreement. He was right, and it reminded me of the list vs. schedule predicament, which Vernon might be able to help me with.

"Plus the way he quoted from the book and talked about that guy who wrote it – Kripanali," Ted went on, "It was like a cult, and the book is his bible." We both laughed nervously. There was some truth to everything he pointed out, and when our laughter stopped, I said, "You're right, buddy, but what can we do?"

He looked down at the carpet and scratched the floor with his foot.

"I'm going to give it a shot," I said, answering my own question. "I need to get better about managing everything coming at me. Too much stuff falls through the cracks, and I need to find a better way. Might as well start there."

"Like the game last week?" he added with a twinkle in his eye. At that moment, I remembered. We had planned to go watch a Knicks game at Madison Square Garden, but it had fallen by the wayside when I forgot to call for tickets in time. I winced in agreement. I remembered that I hadn't even called him to close the loop, and he nodded at me with a smile.

"Yeah, like that."

"Well, I'm all for some improvement in that area," he joked. "I thought about reminding you, but I figured I could bring it up when I needed some points on the board." He made a free-throw action, smoothly sinking an imaginary ball in an invisible hoop.

"Well, it looks like I should take a closer look at what the book says in order to try to use it. I think there's some good stuff in it."

He paused for a moment and then got angry again. "I don't think it's the book I have a problem with. It's jerks like Vermin who believe that their way is the best way while the rest of us deserve to have it rammed down our throats."

"Yup, no disagreement there," I replied. "He's a crazy man, and I don't want to make it look as if I'm giving in to his bullying, but for the sake of the project, let's see what the book says and use it for ourselves."

"He's still a royal pain in the ass," Ted reminded me, even as he nodded grudgingly. "I'll see if I can get the others to jump in also."

That's the easy job, I thought. *Saving my job and becoming more productive isn't an option, it's a requirement.*

---

"By the way," he added as he turned towards to door and paused before leaving, "I hear through the grapevine that there's another layoff coming and that a list is floating around."

My heart stopped beating on a dime, and my mouth felt filled with dust. I held my breath as he paused to run a hand through his hair. Two seconds felt like two days.

"Supposedly, my name is on it. My old supervisor gave me the heads up and told me that I needed to be part of a successful project for a change. I can list 10 projects I have worked on since I joined the company, and not a single one ever ended successfully."

This was true, but it wasn't his fault. Syscon's bureaucracy only allowed the occasional project to escape the quicksand of corporate politics and bungling incompetence.

On the verge of telling him that I was also rumored to be "almost" on the list, I offered, "That sucks, man -- sorry to hear that." Hopefully, he didn't have any bad news to add about my name.

"I know. I guess I'll have to make this project work, or it will be like, no more Ted to kick around." He made a kicking motion, still smooth after his years of collegiate level soccer.

He looked at me for a response, but all I could do was watch his kick sail through the air.

That evening before I got home, I swung by the local Starbucks. Scanning the room as I joined the line for a latte, I noticed a familiar figure. *Stevnellie9612.* It was Joseph, the victim of Syscon's restructuring program and the guy whose job I was told to "do in addition to your own until further notice."

I walked over and tried a little Columbo. "Stevnellie?"

His blank look made me feel very, very stupid. "Oh, hello, Bill. Sorry, I was too deep in my BrainPhone. What did you say about a nelly?"

*So much for my detective skills.*

"Sorry Joseph, I thought you were someone else. Can I join you?" I sat, but not before I noticed that behind his thick glasses, his eyes were filled with tears and his face was a mess. *Oh no.* Just as the rumors said, he was dressed for a day in the office. As a matter of fact, he was over-dressed for Syscon, wearing a crumpled red tie and shabby blue blazer.

I offered lamely, "Are you okay?"

"Yeah, I used to be. But now, things have just gotten tough."

"But I heard that you got some second interviews over at Maytheon Solutions? And that you were right in line to get that job?"

"Yeah, me and about 200 other guys. They told us that they started out with over 1000. This was after I got excited about getting my first callback. That was the last I heard from them."

"What's your plan?" I asked after telling him how sorry I was.

"Well, I met a couple of guys I knew from MIT who were also trying to get that job, and we decided to start our own thing. Two minutes ago, one of them called to bail out. He got a job in Canada. Apparently, they have jobs over there. He was the one with the idea and the money, so...." His voice tailed off.

In the car on the way home, I couldn't think of a single thing that would help him. The pressure he was under was enormous. We promised to keep in touch, but that would hardly pay his bills, save his home, or keep his family from falling into a financial hole.

I turned into my driveway only after making two missed turns. I sat for a minute, looking at Lizzy's bicycle in the garage, thrown down without a care in the middle of the floor. Fighting back a rising feeling of panic, I bit my lip and walked into the house to get a warm welcome from my family. At least we were still okay right now.

* * *

At work the next day, Vernon found me working on my laptop at my cubicle. It was around 9:00 in the morning as I took my first sip of a cup of coffee mixed with cocoa, helped by copious amounts of sugar. Today I was sampling the good stuff - Blue Mountain Supreme from Jamaica - from the local coffee shop, because it was the very best antidote to a day that featured a long slog through DAPE documentation. My brain was still in pre-coffee fog. Awake, but not working so well.

"Good morning," he announced in a cheery voice before skipping over my fumbling reply. "I just finished a five mile run so I'm ready to go. It's time for us to sit down for a quick coaching session."

What was he on about now?

"It won't take long, don't worry. I told Martha I'd give you some extra time and attention, given the challenges you face." Challenges? I struggled to keep a straight face. Inside, I started boiling like the inside of a whistling coffee pot. What exactly did he know? What had she told him?

"I thought I was doing okay so far," I stammered, half-smiling, trying to ease the tension that was creeping into my neck and back.

"Well," he said, "It's not good enough, but I'll tell you what to do. All you have to do is learn." He sat down without waiting for a response.

I badly wanted to talk to him about my scheduling techniques and why I had made the transition from all those lists. However, I let him take the lead.

"I'm really glad you have that BrainPhone, because it makes you more responsive. It's important to be there when management wants you. I respond to emails 24 hours a day, 7 days a week, and I'm getting ahead because I do something that only a few can do. I can act like an executive all the time, and that's how you need to perform."

My insides churned. I disagreed, vehemently. I bit my tongue.

"Just last week I got some email from both Manuel and Nick on the new quality check for DAPE. When I got back to them within minutes, they were impressed. If you want to impress people, one easy way is to be responsive, and there's nothing they like more than an employee who's on top of things. They didn't know at first that I was at my sister's wedding, but I made sure they knew. Now that's being productive. Plus, it's the only way to make it nowadays at Syscon. It's not like the old days, when we could take an hour to get back to people."

"Vernon...Vernon." Starting timidly at first, I got louder until he stopped to listen. I drew in a deep breath.

"To be honest, I'm not doing that. I'm not playing the 24-7 game. I can send you the research that shows that it ruins productivity. I'll only check email once or twice per day. The 24-7 thing simply doesn't work for me, and it's the reason Syscon is implementing new texting and driving policies."

What I said had the same effect as a direct hit of lightning to the middle of his forehead. His mouth dropped open and a fire leapt into his eyes. He drew a sharp intake of air, as if readying himself to lift a 200 pound barbell, and I braced myself.

Then, he closed his eyes.

For about ten seconds, he appeared to be meditating. My mother used to do this to me when I was a kid – I think she counted to ten to stop herself from giving me a good smack around the ears.

When his eyes opened, his face was hard and set in stone. But his eyes were still blazing.

"I don't want you to think this is all about BrainPhone stuff. What's also important is that you improve your time management skills, and I don't think you're following all of the Master Time Method in the way you should. For example, do you have the ten to fifteen lists to work with each day?"

I wasn't ready for that question, so he answered it himself. "Actually, I don't think it matters why. You need to follow the book's practices entirely, or you won't be successful. Xavier Kripanali makes it very, very clear in his book. It's also a requirement for this team's success."

"He does make it clea—"Vernon cut me off again before I could complete the thought or ask the question that was really on my mind.

"Bill, let's be honest. There's not much to talk about here. Either you intend to follow the book or not: yes or no. Which one is it?"

If only he had showed up when I was fully awake. Lost for words and pre-caffeinated, I produced a mumbled "Okay."

That seemed to make him happy. "Great – let's meet to catch up on your progress on Mondays, Wednesdays and Fridays. I'm away on business for the next 2 weeks, so when I get back we can get cracking. You can send me the results from your little research project on smartphones."

And then he was gone. I sat in my chair feeling stunned. My head spun as if I had just come off the Tilt-a-Whirl at the County Fair.

Something was wrong about all this. Very, very wrong. But what?

* * *

Over a ham sandwich at my desk, I thought about Vernon's "coaching." My "little research project." I was feeling pretty raw, smothered and just a bit freaked out. But at least I had put my foot down. Sort of.

The spurt of confidence didn't last long. It wasn't a good thing to be known as the guy who "isn't a team player." Talk about a kiss of death. My refusal to play that particular game could land me in all sorts of hot water.

*What have I done?*

The more I thought about it, the more it looked like a bad mistake. I didn't need to go up against Vernon like that. I could have accepted what he wanted and just patched things up at home with Sandy and the kids. I pictured myself at the dinner table, explaining why Daddy needed to be available at work right now and why he was so important that people wanted to contact him all the time.

I dropped my sandwich in the plate. Why hadn't I thought of that? As I reached for my bottle of water, some of it spilled onto my keyboard. I carefully set it aside as my trembling hands formed fists. My jaw tightened.

What exactly had Martha told him about my situation? Did she tell him that I was in trouble? If he knew, then I was stupid to fight him like that. All he had to do was wait me out while gradually tightening the screws to keep me in line. My own fears of ending up on that list would do the rest.

*How the hell can I get out of this?*

To make things worse, I was about to have a hell of a time following the book. Vernon wasn't going to be happy until we were all goose-stepping and saluting the MTM flag. This was no Cub Scout outing in the woods. I Googled Hogan's Heroes. Just for fun.

# Chapter 5

===========================
**Bill Crossley**
-----------------------------------------------
From: Bill.Crossley@syscon.com
To: Vernon.Vaz@syscon.com
BCC: Martha.Adelman@syscon.com, Ted.Brewster@syscon.com
Subject: Smartphone Abuse

Hi Vernon,

As promised, here is the data I gathered on smartphone abuse.

- 25% think that their supervisors expect them to be online/connected after hours
- 15% plan to attend one or more work-related calls or web meetings during their next vacation
- 17% say it's frowned upon to be unavailable during vacations
62% check work email over the weekend, and 19% check it five or more times in a weekend
- 19% check email before getting out of bed
- 78% check email on vacation
- 72% check email outside working hours
- 42% check email on sick days
- 69% agreed that owning a smartphone, laptop of other mobile device has increased the number of hours they work each week

There is also a raft of data that shows that multi-tasking is unproductive. Employees only spend 11 minutes on average on a task before being interrupted. It takes 25 minutes to become productive after being interrupted, or after switching to a new task. When we multitask we create an "illusion of competence."

As I said, it doesn't work for me to be available 24-7. I tried it and found that it actually produced some bad habits that I am trying to unlearn, in keeping with Syscon's new policy on texting and driving.

I am keen to adopt practices that boost my time management skills and expand my productivity, but this doesn't appear to be one of them. I welcome any data to the contrary.

Also, I'm moving forward to implement MTM to its fullest extent.

Regards,

Bill
---------------------------------------------

After I clicked <Send>, I felt a little better, so I continued by opening a new note on my BrainPhone.

After visiting the MTM site for a few details, I summarized the differences between my current habits and the ones described in MTM.

MTM
- Keep multiple to-do lists of stuff to do sorted by priority, location and urgency
- Review these lists regularly
- Sync these lists with my BrainPhone

Bill's Method
- Keep a single schedule/calendar
- Sync it with my BrainPhone

It seemed simple enough on paper. Now all I needed to do was reverse ten years of consistent practice. Right away. Stop putting stuff in my calendar and start putting it all on lists.

I sat back, staring at the ceiling, trying to remember how I actually started deviating from MTM's rules.

My mind flashed back to Florida, where I had earned a quick promotion to supervisor right after Lizzy was born. Then came 9/11, and our business went crazy. We did back-office operations for insurance companies and had to process benefits for hundreds of workers who had been killed or sickened by the tragedy. We helped thousands of New Yorkers get back on their feet quickly.

An advanced program in project management gave me the initial spark, but it was my own idea to use a single schedule instead of a bunch of lists. That turned into a lifesaver when we were forced to become a six- and sometimes seven-day-a-week operation, just to keep up with the sudden volume of work.

My experience contradicted Xavier, who was quite clear on this point. The only way to be effective was to practice making lists and to keep a bare bones calendar. Other options were inefficient, he stated bluntly.

But why?

I scoured the Internet and his eBook for some justification for this position. Apparently, back in the mid-1990's, he tried to use a single paper schedule and found that it didn't work as well as keeping multiple lists, also on paper. That was it. He broadened that single experience to claim that it wouldn't work for anyone, at any time. Everything was anecdotal; he hadn't done any research.

*The 1990's?* People were still using big fat binders with those pages you had to purchase at the local office store. I'd had one too.

Trusting a hunch, I dug a bit deeper to try to find what kind of academic research actually existed. Sure enough, I discovered some evidence compiled by Dezhi Wu, a brilliant researcher from the University of Southern Utah. Her book's title was long: *Temporal Structures in Individual Time Management: Practices to Enhance Calendar Tool Design.* It described how the best time managers used their calendars to plan out their time. Her background as a software designer indicated that she knew a lot about project planning tools and how to use them. Her book applied that knowledge to individual calendar use in a groundbreaking way.

At the same time, Xavier was right about most things, especially when it came to people's tendency to try to trust their memories. Using memory only worked for people whose lives were simple, like teenagers.

When they grew to become young adults, he said, they started to experience the limits of using memory. After they got married, started having kids, or accepted a promotion, things would start to go crazy. Methods that previously worked well would fall apart, because they couldn't memorize that much stuff. At Syscon, this was true - it was the younger whipper-snappers who got into trouble when their memories failed them.

All these questions were intriguing, but this was about survival, not academic interest.

Using the book, I started to set up the lists. I went into my calendar and stripped out all the items that didn't require other people's attendance. Some of the things that remained in my schedule included:
- Meetings at work, such as DAPE updates
- My dental appointment
- The next date night with Sandy

Taking about two hours, I converted my calendar (my former control center) back into a simple appointment calendar.

Things that were removed and added to my new lists included:

- Time spent at the gym
- Scheduled work on deliverables for projects like DAPE
- Reminders to pay bills
- Set times each week to go shopping
- All the one-off action items that I had decided to complete

It left a lot of empty space behind, which made it look as if I had lots of spare time. For once, I was glad that we didn't share calendars in Outlook, because my colleagues would assume that I had all this free time when I actually didn't.

My life hadn't changed one bit, but the way it was represented had.

Was this an improvement? Now I'd have to remember to pay bills on time, remind myself to go to the gym, and try not to forget to start work early on DAPE deliverables.

Near the end of this exercise, which took the better part of the afternoon, I got some email from Ted. He was still excited about the idea of taking our families on an exotic Caribbean cruise. We still had to find out the options, pick one, coordinate schedules, get the payment together, apply for passports, etc. He asked me to set some time aside to help him check things out in the next two weeks.

Reflexively, I turned on my BrainPhone and almost had a heart attack when I saw wide open days in my calendar. *Where did my stuff go?* Then, I remembered... *You just took it out.*

How could I tell if I had enough time to do the research Ted needed? Inside, I groaned. The only thing I could do was to take a guess.

That didn't feel like an improvement - not in my gut. But that's exactly what I did.

"Time to shut up and be a team player," I muttered while shooting him a reply.

* * *

On Friday morning, I attended a kick-off meeting, chaired by Manuel, to plan the development of a department vision and mission statement. Apparently, the managers in our division felt it was time to rally the troops in a common cause, which happened to be something I had complained about for over a year. I listened as he laid out the reasons for the project.

"We focus too much on cost-cutting around here. That's no way to accomplish greatness. I am hoping that we can use this effort to help change our culture of holding into a culture of springing forward. You get me?"

Coming from Manuel, with his full white, business-man's haircut and grave bearing, we could tell this was important.

We only had a chance to ask a few questions before he turned to me with his piercing blue eyes. "Bill, I'd like you to lead up the Mission Team."

It was an offer I couldn't refuse and didn't want to. It was a spotlight position, and if I did a good job, it would raise my stocks. "Sure," I responded as others nodded their heads in encouragement.

"Are you sure you have the time?" he added. I cut him off before he could go any further.

"Hang on a minute so I can check. We'd need to meet for one day each week, at least."

"It has to be Fridays," he reminded me, "due to travel schedules." Everyone nodded in agreement.

I clicked on my BrainPhone and opened up the calendar - from habit. Once again, it was empty and I almost had another panic attack until I remembered that I was now working with lists. I scoured my mind to remember what the next six to eight weeks looked like, and when I was pretty sure there was some free time, I announced, "I'm good to go."

An hour later, I found a blue covered document with a note from Vernon on my desk. I opened up an outline of key DAPE deliverables - something we had been working on for a few weeks. I flipped over to my page to make sure it was kosher.

Staring back at me, I found the promises I had made earlier in the month to deliver some important items and their dates. The plan called for two solid days of solo work on my part for the next two months, starting in a couple of weeks. One of those days had to be a Friday because of the Monday morning status meetings we had planned. These personal work days had been sitting in my calendar, but not anymore. Now, those days looked clear, but they certainly weren't.

With my heart beating fast, I typed "Sorry, Manuel, but my workload won't permit me to lead the team. Actually, I can't see how I can even be a member, given my commitments."

When I hit <Return>, the beat slowed down, and I couldn't stop it from sinking. Manuel wouldn't say anything, but he was sure to think it.

* * *

It was a bad start.

On Monday, two weeks after the fiasco with Manuel, I sat down to search for other people who had made the switch from a single schedule to MTM-style lists. Nothing came up. The problem preyed on my mind during the afternoon coaching session with Vernon.

Once again, he talked and I listened. I tried to get in a few words but I still felt as if I were his congregation of one as he cajoled me to follow "The Master Time Method" in all its glory. He dismissed all of my tentative queries with an appropriate quote. Thankfully, his skill at answering his own questions made the session short.

After our session, I continued my search for answers using Google. I found many of avid MTM users on LinkedIn and Facebook. A few were hard-core fans like Vernon who would allow no deviation from Xavier's writings. They didn't take lightly to people who asked too many uncomfortable questions, making me sometimes feel like a Republican at a Democratic fundraiser.

One recurring complaint from these groups was one that I shared, and I nodded my head each time I ran into it on the Internet. Because MTM called for the placement of all action items in multiple to-do lists, it required the user to implement "Regular Scans." By definition, this scan involved a check of all the items in every single list, to make sure that nothing would ever fall through the cracks. Kripanali's system gave the user an option to choose the scans' frequency: daily, twice per week, weekly, fortnightly, monthly. It was one of the few choices he provided his readers.

Unfortunately, it didn't seem to matter. Users reported that they suffered through the tedium of their Regular Scans, even though they knew MTM wouldn't work without them. When I reread the book, the scans seemed to make perfect sense. In actual practice, however, I quickly began to hate them, even though they seemed to be unavoidable. Without them, responsibilities would simply get lost.

A blogger specializing in lifehacks explained the reason why. A Regular Scan is actually a mental snapshot of what you have to do between scans: a calendar stored in your memory. If you have a relatively low number of to-dos, it's not too difficult.

The lifehacker explained, "People who have a lot of items on their lists find the review to be repetitious. They don't like going over the same lists of the same things over and over again. When they attempt to form a mental calendar, they suffer, because there is simply too much information to remember."

The post resonated with me. It was important to have this mental calendar ready so that when Martha, for example, asked about my availability to complete a project, I could give her an answer. During easy weeks, this wasn't hard, but in a heavy week it was just a killer. There was no easy way to remember a complex, multi-day sequence of activities.

In the book, the scan was treated as an easy and logical part of MTM. Out here in the real world, it proved to be a major time hog.

Was this really better than keeping a detailed schedule? Now, I had more to commit to memory, and there was little comfort in realizing that I wasn't alone. All Xavier would say in response to the complaints – people needed to "discipline themselves."

As a sanity check, I took a look at some less popular time management and productivity books, but they all marched to the same tune. Make lots of to-do lists. Manage them all at the same time. Do frequent reviews. Don't use your calendar for anything other than appointments. Keep reviewing these lists to make sure that nothing slips off your radar. Be disciplined. Not a single writer backed the calendar-based approach I was leaving behind, so I started to wonder if I wasn't a little crazy.

About a week later, I received an email newsletter from a guy who signed his name "G." He had completed a comparison of the major time management books. According to him, their authors hadn't kept up with the times, which meant their helpful new technology wasn't being used.

More specifically, they could now replace a bunch of to-do lists with a single, fully portable electronic schedule. He said that a calendar was nothing more than a "rich-text list," or a list of to-dos with dates on each item, sorted by date. When he quoted Dezhi Wu's work, I perked up.

He described three transitions that people typically made. The first was from using memory to using a single to-do list. The second was from a single list to multiple to-do lists. The third took place when they replaced multiple to-do lists with a single electronic calendar or schedule. (He used the words 'calendar' and 'schedule' interchangeably.) They made these jumps out of desperation and not because they were taught to do so in a class.

"The amount of information they have to process each day grows to the point where their current approach starts to fail, and they need to change their tactics." These three transitions were their self-created attempts to get better.

He also cited other research showing that many college students were already using calendars in the most effective way, enabled by smartphone and tablet technology. Unfortunately, when they left school, it seemed as if they abandoned their good habits and reverted to using memory because their first jobs were usually nowhere as demanding as their final semesters.

When I completed his paper, I leaned back in my chair and looked up at the ceiling with my hands interlocked behind my neck. From head to toe, my muscles stretched and then relaxed. *No, I wasn't alone.*

A few minutes later I was scrolling through G's website. His real name was Graham Riley and he lived in Ithaca, New York, home of Cornell University. Sure enough, he lectured at the school as an adjunct.

This was all intellectually interesting, I summarized as I closed down G's website. What difference would it make if what I needed to do was follow MTM by the book? Sure, I'd used something else in the past, but I needed to buckle down and do what Vernon asked.

Once again, that nagging feeling that something wasn't right wouldn't go away, but once again I shoved it aside. I would have time later to check out G and his stuff, but for now, that just couldn't be a priority. As we entered early November, some challenging weeks were coming up on the DAPE project. The evenings were already getting longer, and it was time to "hunker down" and keep things quiet until the spring. Then, maybe, I could muck around with some of this new stuff.

* * *

Just as I had predicted, during the remaining weeks of November the project picked up in intensity.

DAPE was in a critical phase in which the prototypes we developed would be tested by select employees - an exercise that amounted to an internal beta test of sorts. This intense period promised long hours and hard work to respond to user input, fix the problems, and make the prototypes available again in a few days for retesting.

In one of the meetings during the first week, Manuel and Martha sat in on a briefing. As they listened to our presentations, Martha interjected, "I think you are missing some checkpoints -- we used to call them Quality Gates in the old days. We need to have one in place right after the first round of testing is completed."

Manuel added, "I agree -- it would help to make sure that we're on track with the findings of the initial tests."

Vernon agreed. "No problem, I'll make sure that we get it done." He looked over in my direction, making it clear that I'd be the one to get the Quality Gate set up. I asked "How about November 10th?" and in a few minutes we had agreed that the date would be ideal.

Over the next few days, a tremendous number of additional tasks arose from a number of meetings. We all wanted the prototype testing phase to go well, given how important the project was to the company. It felt good to have everyone on board, moving in the right direction.

A couple of days later, Vernon gave me a call. "We need to change the date of that Quality Gate -- it's coming too early in the process and we won't have the data we need."

I agreed and answered, "Let's move it to the 15th." He concurred. "Let me be the one to tell Martha and Manuel so that they know why we're doing this. You go ahead and tell the team, then update the project schedule."

On the evening of November 9th, I was at home watching television alone when I heard my phone ring. It was a call from Martha, which was unusual, as she knew that I was trying not to answer my BP at night. I lowered the volume on Law and Order, my favorite show, and clicked over to the call.

She immediately apologized for calling so late. "But I need to know -- what time is the Quality Gate meeting tomorrow?"

My mind froze, and I stumbled. Did I forget to do something? "That date was moved, Martha -- it's now set for the 15th."

"But it clearly states that it's the 10th on the schedule!"

I winced. I had forgotten to update the project calendar, but the entire team knew that the date had been changed - I had made sure of that via email.

"Sorry Martha -- I should have updated the schedule. I've just been so busy that I forgot."

What I really wanted to say was "My Regular Scans have been killing me, and this single item, faithfully placed on one of my 10 to-do lists, was simply forgotten."

"Vernon was..." I stopped there, not wanting to blame him openly, even though he had promised to update both Martha and Manuel. He'd obviously failed to do what he was supposed to. "It's just a mix-up in communication," I offered.

She took a moment and then said, "Okay, Bill, just make sure that Manuel knows."

I immediately sent an email and text to Vernon to give him a heads up. "Get back to me," I pressed. After half an hour of waiting, I called, but it went straight to voicemail. I wasn't sure what to do, but I knew that I had to get to Manuel before 9:00 am, the original start of the meeting.

Early the next morning, I got up to check email to see if Vernon had received my messages. There was one from him entitled "Meeting Protocols" along with a PDF attachment and a short message, "Please see the attached letter."

I almost ignored it, believing that it had nothing to do with the more urgent matter at hand, but I went ahead and clicked it open on my BP. It was written in tiny print, and I had to squint to see what it said.
=========================
**Vernon Vaz**
-------------------------------------------
From: Vernon.Vaz@syscon.com
To: William.Crossley@syscon.com
cc: Martha.Adelman@yscon.com, Manuel.Bonares@syscon.com
Subject: Your Performance

Dear Mr. Crossley,

It has come to my attention that you have failed, once again, to manage your time well enough to execute your essential duties.

In future, please make sure to advise all meeting attendees of changes to our schedule in keeping with the company's standard meeting protocols. I am available to provide you any coaching that you might need to improve your standard of performance.

Regards

Vernon Vaz
Project Manager - DAPE

---------------------------------------

That... asshole.

I don't normally swear. But this time, I did. Out aloud.

"Honey, what's wrong?" Sandy came into the living room where I sat in my easy chair, a look of dread on her face. Her face and voice were cloudy from interrupted sleep. I caught myself and cut my emotions short.

"Nothing, Honey, just some work stuff," I muttered. When she stood staring at me in disbelief, I quickly added "Just a misunderstanding. I'll take care of it when I go in."

She didn't budge. Her face filled with dark concern, blended with a soft warmth in her eyes that instantly put a heavy lump in my throat. All of a sudden, I wanted to tell her everything. *Damn Dr. Roma.* Having my wife by my side would put us together in fighting the nonsense that I was now dealing with at work.

Before I could get over my thoughts, she sighed and walked away. *What was I thinking?* To risk getting her into this mess when it was still so crazy and uncertain? Perplexed, I sat there unmoving. Right thing? Wrong thing? No clue.

My mind jolted back to Vernon... Now, I knew why he had earned that damned nickname: Vermin. He'd just sold me out over a mistake on his part.

*What the hell should I do about this?*

# Chapter 6

Two weeks later, I was still walking around in a daze.

My body showed up at work, but that was about it, as my mind stayed in a world of its own, running like a hamster on a wheel, going over the incident with Vernon again and again. That week's Regular Scan was an awful affair.

These sessions were now the low point of the week. Going over 10 long agendas that I had already done or needed to do week after week exhausted me. I sorely missed the simplicity of managing my calendar. Each time I sat down to do these reviews, Vernon's voice echoed, "Xavier Kripanali says that..." Then, I'd recall Sandy's comment about doing stupid things just because other people did them.

This week's review was torture with the fresh memory of Vernon's email - a cyber-stab in the back.

On the phone with Ted one morning, he asked me how things were going.

"Vernon's letter? Haven't forgotten it, no. My inner Gandhi is yet to emerge. I still want to kill the guy, if that's what you mean."

"But who cares what he does? Why is it so important? It's just another project here at Syscon -- there will be others."

So I told him. About the email, the list, Martha's warning. Vernon's "help." "You're not Stevnellie in disguise are you?"

He laughed. "Sorry this is happening -- it sounds awful. What now?"

"Well -- I'm truly on my own here. Vernon is doing his best to avoid me. Probably afraid that I'll go to Martha to complain. I'm not going to whine to her, but I have written my share of poisonous emails and saved them to my hard drive in case I ever go postal."

"Just don't leave the company with your email files intact. At my wife's company, some lady left her Outlook folders undeleted and the guys in I.T. had a ball reading her juicy emails to three boyfriends. None to her husband by the way."

He didn't mean to push me over the edge, but the phrase "leave the company" was all that was needed.

"Speaking of leaving the company, how is your job search going?" Ted had been trying to move to North Jersey for a couple of years, and he'd sent his resume to a number of potential employers.

"Awful -- there's a recession on, you know," he said with a hint of sadness in his voice. "I won't give up, but it's not looking pretty. One interview in 12 months, and only because I knew the guy from college. Why? Are you looking too? I guess Vernon has gotten to you." Ted had predicted that he would "get" to all of us eventually and that we'd end up as his miserable serfs. It was hilarious at the time, but I wasn't laughing now.

"Well... yeah." I responded wearily.

"Okay," he said with a new, serious tone, "most local engineering firms like Syscon are actually looking to reduce headcount, not increase it. Bad time to be looking... did you hear the talk about a jobless recovery?"

I had pointedly ignored that particular headline. "Any news about Joseph and his search?"

"Yeah, there's news. Here are the headlines: Man Moves Family in with Parents. Finds New Career at Subway. Wife Splits Charging In-Law Harassment. Should I keep going?"

"Hell, no. Poor Joseph."

I hung up with Ted, then clicked onto Monster.com and some other job search sites. They confirmed what he had said, just as I expected. There were almost no jobs in this area, not even for engineers with advanced degrees. My heart sunk. 2010 wasn't 2005. When I had moved from Florida back to New Jersey, there were lots of jobs for people like me. Back then, Syscon had welcomed me back with open arms.

There was no way this was going to stop me, so I broadened my search to include resume boards and online classified ads. Every day up until Thanksgiving, I checked and rechecked, stopping only when Sandy insisted that we put away all electronic devices for the day.

Ted was right in one respect. "You should be thankful; at least you have a job today and your next paycheck is a sure thing. That's a lot more than you can say for lots of other people who are searching," he said during our conversation. He was right, and on Turkey Day, I followed some advice from the Today Show and wrote a list of all of the things I should be grateful for.

After doing the exercise, I decided to hang tough and focus on being thankful for the good things in my life. That got me through the holiday weekend, and I wanted to make my family happy for the first time in months. Mom and Dad, who had visited us a couple times, even said that I looked to be in good shape. Sure, I was hiding stuff from them and from Sandy, but the exercise seemed to be working and I felt a little better.

When I arrived at work on Monday after the long weekend, a new announcement popped up: "Reorganizing for Success."

* * *

My eyes flashed with fear and I could barely read or breathe. I hurriedly scanned the announcement. I read it once, twice, and a few more times to be sure; then I sat back when I had made sure I was safe.

Gone were 11 people, including Val Smith, who had been working with us on the DAPE project. She was a single mother who had an MBA from Columbia and seemed to be pulling her weight on the project.

On the other hand, I recalled a few of Vernon's comments over the past month. He used a couple of Val's mistakes as "teachable moments" in his group coaching. "Well," I muttered, "I guess she's learned her lesson."

The others who were being forced to go were people whom I didn't know so well. A guy in his forties. A female engineer. The older fellow who sat by himself in the lunch room. Others I couldn't immediately place.

The announcement was made with the usual corporate-speak that you find everywhere, and it claimed that this sad headline resulted from each person's desire to "seek other opportunities."

A sick sense of relief seeped over me, a little like the feeling you get when you see a car crash and realize that no one you know was in it. I felt a pang of guilt when I reminded myself that Val had two daughters, just like I did. In fact, they went to Lizzy's school.

Then, I recalled a sentence at the bottom of the announcement. I scrolled through the message until I found it, "Syscon is committed to continuing its right-sizing effort and expects another announcement to be made by the end of the year."

"Enough," I whispered. Bypassing my MTM lists, I opened up Monster.com and started putting the final touches on my online resume. Within a few minutes, I made my resume visible and started searching Monster for any job I could find between DC and Maine.

By the time the first chilly Monday morning in December rolled around, my resume was whizzing through the Internet to three companies for jobs that I knew I couldn't get. But at least I was trying.

On my way to lunch, I checked my email in the elevator and saw a message from Martha, asking for a meeting. It was short, cold and to the point. Very unlike her. "Big.... or small?" I wondered aloud as my heart began to pound, anticipating the worst. In the past week, a number of closed door meetings around the office made me think that something was up. My Tzinbox score of -9 didn't do much to lighten up my mood, and for the first time, I had seriously considered turning the feature off.

I sat in her office as she finished typing, seemingly distracted. Then she looked me right in the face. "Bill, I know that you have been on the DAPE Project for only a few months, but something urgent has come up. We're going to ask you to leave."

* * *

I stared at her as my knees lost their strength and my mind went blank. A few days before Christmas - *this was not happening.*

She must have noticed my facial expression as it dropped to the floor, and she smiled mischievously.

"Whoops... that didn't come out well. Don't panic -- you aren't losing your job! We have an urgent need for you to spend a year with a firm that we are thinking of partnering with. It's called RingCORE -- remember them?"

I nodded my head, not only to signal my agreement but also to shake off the shock of her opening words, which had set my heart pumping and eyes blinking all on their own. I drew some deep breaths, not caring if she thought I was a wuss.

"Our CEOs have been talking, and they want to get someone over there who knows the Zebon technology. Plus, we want to know more about their game platform and how we can apply it to our own products. You spoke with them over the summer, right?"

"Yeah - an impressive bunch of guys."

"Well, it would mean working with them full-time for about twelve months. We'll extend it if we see an opportunity for mutual benefit."

My eyebrows shot up. This was exactly how they had gotten rid of Anna...seconded to some outfit in California, then never brought back.

I nodded. It was all I could do at the moment. At the same time, I could see some light against the dark, Vernon-style management. Twelve months away on an assignment could mean a long timeout from the risk of losing my job. Or was it Anna revisited?

"This isn't a fancy way to let go of old Bill, is it? After all, you won't have me to kick around anymore..." I tried hard not to plead, even as I played around with Nixon's parting shot, so often used by Ted.

"Absolutely not," she replied, taking care to look me straight in the eye. "Your job here is assured while you are gone, and we promise it will be here when you return. You'll still be working here one half-day every two weeks. While you're there, we'll be sharing your payroll with RingCORE, 50-50. Nick likes that part because it helps him meet his headcount target for next year."

I paused for a moment to digest everything. There was good news in this: I would no longer be on the DAPE Project, no longer have to work with Vernon, and I'd actually be "safe" for a whole year. Maybe, if I did a good job, I could get an offer from these guys at RingCORE, assuming that the company behind the strange meeting practices was as sound as it seemed.

There was no real hesitation on my part. "When do I start?"

# Chapter 7

Naturally, I Googled RingCORE as soon as I got back to my cubicle. What were they all about?

They had an awesome website that actually looked designed for a company that had been launched that morning. It had all the latest doodahs, from Flash animation to an up-to-date blog with videos, audios and links to Facebook and Linkedin. At Syscon, we still thought "social" was something you did on weekends with your friends at football games, so we hadn't even set up a Facebook page.

RingCORE was alive with continuous chatter on all its social channels, with thoughts and opinions flying between employees, customers and vendors: anyone who had an interest in discussing the company and its products. They were all excited about the gaming platforms they were creating, and I could see from the online discussions that there was a growing interest in using what they had learned to help college students. That's where we come in, I surmised.

As a cutting-edge software company located in nearby Edison, it was staffed with an army of 20-Somethings who looked as if they had come straight out of the garage, with lots of caps and T-shirts. This was all a far cry from Syscon, with its button-down collars and older engineers.

But the company was no slouch, as I could see. Just because they were young didn't mean that they were ineffective. Far from it. Apparently, their founder, Andre Anderson, was a real productivity nut, and a few articles that outlined their innovative approach to meetings - the things I'd noticed – had been published in various journals. They favored fast, short commonsense meetings. Everyone actually used those home-grown methods; they didn't just talk about them.

*OK, this was exciting.* I leaned back in my chair and looked up at the ceiling. Maybe this could be more than an escape from "Sysca-traz," and I could actually learn a thing or two while there. Stuff that could save my job. I could use this opportunity to decide whether or not I even have a future at Syscon.

I remembered a word I'd bookmarked in my brain: "Sweatshop." I Googled the words "sweatshop" + "RingCORE" and up came the results. Apparently there was a lot of chatter on this topic. The first result referenced a site, which I clicked into. Up came www.ihatethering.com which turned out to be a blog entitled "I Hate RingCORE."

My hands shook just a little as I scrolled down the screen to find a collective exposé written by ex-RingCORE employees. The hundreds of contributors to the site had a lot of bad things to say that could be summarized in the sentence, "It was hell."

* * *

During the holidays, I couldn't shake RingCORE's haters. I tried hard to stay away from the website, but my curiosity got the better of me. When I revisited its messages, I noticed that the most recent entry had taken place a full eleven months prior, indicating that perhaps the anger had subsided. Other ex-employee sites with far fewer bitter feelings helped me pull together a more nuanced story.

Apparently, in 2003, the company had exploded with projects related to games based on the Iraq and Afghanistan wars. They successfully sold them on multiple platforms, but as the work piled on, they pushed employees to work longer hours. This worked for a while until many reached the breaking point, taking sick and work-from-home days to keep their sanity. Lots of good people left in disgust. Management just couldn't control all the new projects, even when it was obvious that they couldn't bring on enough new people to keep up.

After a week of browsing other RingCORE sites, I called it quits. With Christmas around the corner, I didn't want to ruin the time my family had set aside to take a good, long break from the stresses of the year. Plus, it was the first time in months that I didn't feel alone and desperate.

Sandy was happy with the assignment once I explained that it would have little impact on my hours or commute. She'd have been way more concerned if I had told her about the layoff list, because I was, in fact, breaking a cardinal rule - during a layoff, keep your visibility high. Anna had broken that rule, and she had paid the price.

On the first Saturday morning of the New Year, I took Lizzy over to her class at Ken's Karate School. It was the week before reporting to work at RingCORE, so my attention kept returning to my new assignment.

Lizzy was chattering away nervously from the front seat as I tried my best to pay full attention. She was about to do her first Karate exam, and hopefully she'd be carrying a new yellow belt home in just a few hours.

The dojo was located in a strip mall storefront that looked like it used to belong to a restaurant. Now, it was simply an empty space with mats, mirrors and practice equipment. On the wall was a display with belts arrayed in a long row from top to bottom.

I sat down in one of the plastic chairs placed against the wall: the holding pen for nervous parents. Lizzy went straight into her warm-up routine with the other kids and seemed right at home. I watched as an older group of ten potential Brown Belts approached the end of their examination with the Sensei. The smell of their sweat was in the air and their shouts helped keep even the most jaded moms and dads awake.

As I watched them being tested, they each repeated what appeared to me to be identical routines. Only their body language after the routine, along with the Sensei's expression, gave me a clue that some were passing while others were failing. Clearly, they could see some critical differences that I couldn't. The fact was, I knew nothing about Karate apart from a few martial arts movies I had watched as a teen. Also, Lizzy had tried to teach me the fundamentals in the living room. The amount she had learned in a short time was impressive.

When her group started its exam, she joined fifteen other students in a series of kata. Some of the moves they were asked to perform matched those of the prior group, but now I could see a world of difference in technique between them. I couldn't quite put it into words... but the gap was obvious.

However, the Sensei seemed to be just as happy with the progress of this group. On the whole, they were younger, but he seemed genuinely pleased.

Quickly, my mind flashed over to Vernon - why was he so unhappy that I wasn't following MTM the way he wanted? Why couldn't he accept that I had found a different way that worked better for me? He was no expert in implementing MTM - I knew that from the number of mistakes he made. The entire fiasco with the scheduled dates wouldn't have happened if he had advised Manuel and Martha about the changes as he was supposed to. I wasn't an expert either, but he was trying hard to become perfect at it, while I had mixed feelings.

Why couldn't he be like the Sensei, who was happy for the Black Belts, the White Belts and every other belt in between?

Between Lizzy's exam and her promotion ceremony, I picked up a Karate magazine from a side table that advertised an interesting article about the famous movie star, Bruce Lee. He was not only a great actor, but also an innovator, creating his very own system of martial arts called Jeet Kune Do. That made me stop to think.

What if I had the desire to go off and create my own version of MTM? It could be "MTM 2.0" or "Bill's New Thing." Shouldn't Vernon, or even Xavier, be happy about that, if I could show that it was better?

I had a feeling Vernon wouldn't exactly welcome that particular breakthrough; it would be like running off to start my own religion. Instead, he was fixated on getting me to execute MTM exactly as the book defined it. The only effort to be made was to follow its prescriptions to the letter. Not just by me, but by everyone at Syscon.

When I thought of everyone doing the same thing, exactly the same way, over and over again, I smiled. The image of goose-stepping stormtroopers popped back in. Imagine getting stuck in the middle of a march and deciding you wanted to do something different or be somewhere else.

And then it struck me... "Getting Stuck"....that's exactly what the Master Time Method was trying to do. Stick me with a particular belt. A low-ranked one like yellow, but certainly not orange or green.

My thoughts about Karate belts were interrupted by a lady not too far from me who was having a frantic conversation with her son. He was also taking the exam to earn a yellow belt, and he obviously didn't want to be there. Almost on the verge of tears, he wanted nothing to do with a Karate exam. I couldn't hear his mother, who was whispering fiercely into his ear, which was no more than an inch away.

"All I want to do is play...!" That's what he cried nine or ten times, jumping in whenever she paused for a breath. After about ten minutes of this, she decided that she'd had enough and dragged him out of Ken's Karate School. He wasn't earning his yellow belt today; that was for sure. I caught the eye of another father sitting nearby, who shook his head and said, "Everyone earns the belt they need and no more."

I nodded in agreement and repeated the thought to myself, "Everyone earns the time management system they need and no more." They don't get a black belt in time management if they don't need one. They don't use the Master Time Method if they don't need it. They might need something better than Xavier's system. Or something worse. Or something in between. They need what they need.

What's more, their needs may change over time.

I thought about that kid who had just left. He might be happy for 30 years, showing off the White Belt he got for simply signing up for the class. At age 40, in a mid-life crisis, he might decide to return to Ken's to continue his training. But for now, he might only want a White Belt. Who could say he was wrong?

By contrast, there were lots of stories on television of kids who were about Lizzy's age and had earned black belts. This was unimaginable. My precious little Lizzy, being that serious about anything, let alone her self-defense skills? She obviously didn't want or need a black belt in any discipline right now. All she wanted was to be a kid and play on the swings, which still happened to be her favorite fun activity. When she played on that thing, hours could pass. That was the way that we all should enjoy whatever we do, with full abandon and without a care in the world.

Staring intently at Lizzy's group, I picked out a kid going through his yellow belt exam. He was "into it" in a kind of effortless way that was interesting to watch. It didn't appear to my untrained eye as if he was trying hard; he was doing each of the kata smoothly with a kind of single-minded purpose that set him apart from the others. True, he was a year or two older than Lizzy, but he was enjoying Karate as much as she enjoyed playing on the swings.

He didn't have an overbearing parent forcing him to do something he didn't want to do. His Dad was watching happily, but not doing much from the benches where we sat. The kid just seemed lost in doing something he loved.

Wasn't that the point? He was being productive and fulfilled.

I could see it more clearly now - people didn't need MTM or any other single method. Unlike Karate, which had to be learned from an instructor, most people taught themselves their own time management methods, like little Bruce Lees. Every single working adult had to manage time with some collection of unconscious habits. The system they used might not have a name or an acronym, but it certainly was their creation. It got them to work on time, helped them pay their bills, balanced their lives, helped keep them healthy... they had to be using something if they functioned as adults with full-time jobs along with all their personal and financial obligations.

For some reason, my math class with my favorite grade-school teacher, Miss Millson popped into mind. She had taught me in the 8th grade at Edison Middle School. She never once told us that 8th Grade Math was all we needed. Far from it - she talked about us getting PhD's and Master's Degrees in math. But, for some students who dropped out of school a few years later, it was the last of the subject they ever learned. Once again, to each his own.

My thoughts quickened. I grabbed a pad from the table and borrowed a pen to start scribbling some notes.

If it was true that people had their own systems of self-created practices by the time they were in their early twenties, then it was no wonder they struggled when they picked up the MTM book later in life, just as I had. It didn't acknowledge that something was already in place that worked pretty well.

Sensei and Miss Millson made it clear that what they were teaching at any point in time was a single set of skills among a wide range. From white to black belt. From first grade to the PhD. They didn't allow anyone to "Get Stuck" at one level or rung. They were also okay if a learner decided not to go further up the ladder.

With Vernon's "help," I was actually taking a step down the ladder, by reversing some of the improvements I'd made over the years. Vernon didn't see or allow that - the MTM rung was the final rung, as far as he was concerned. He was wrong. I just knew it.

A better teaching method would help someone understand where they currently were on the ladder of skills and what they needed to do to move to the next step. Up, not down. This put their attention in the right place: what they could do to get better. All the attention that I wasted on trying to follow MTM perfectly was simply... garbage.

A thrill rose inside me as I watched the Sensei work with his students.

The answer to making improvements in time management didn't lie in finding something outside us, but in understanding ourselves. That was the first step. Maybe the second step was figuring out where we wanted to be. Once we could see the gaps, it should be easier to fill them. Only then would MTM or a smartphone make sense - once we knew what we wanted to change.

I turned this idea over and over in my mind, looking for gaps in the logic. I kept reminding myself that Karate was unlike time management because people didn't normally teach themselves a martial art before coming to their first class. At the same time, I could see right in front of me that kids were picking up new moves more quickly than adults were.

If people knew that they already had a time management system in place, maybe they'd be smarter about using books like MTM. Maybe if Xavier knew this, he'd address the obvious fact that I had seen on the ground at Syscon - most people were "failing" to follow MTM, and many felt guilty. I knew this by looking around at the DAPE team.

At this point, several weeks after our awful first meeting, everyone had read Xavier Kripanali's book. Our team members were all over the map in how they were using it. To me, it seemed crazy to think that we'd all end up with the same habits and practices at the end of the day, even if we wanted to. As adult human beings, it was just too hard to make deeply ingrained habits into a uniform, shared whole.

Perhaps MTM and all the other books had it wrong, and there was no one-size-fits-all way to be productive. I wrote this down on my pad and tore off the paper. Tired, but still excited.

When Lizzy and I left a few minutes later, my head was spinning and I felt almost giddy. She wore her new yellow belt while I wore a slight grin. But I was also puzzled and couldn't let go of a question... was I the only person who had discovered the obvious truth about time management?

* * *

Back at home, we celebrated Lizzy's achievement with a meal of Chicken McNuggets topped with barbecue and sweet-and-sour sauce. Mixed together. In that precise order. After the kids had gone off to play, Sandy handed me another letter from the bank. The annoyed look on her face told me everything. Once again, up went our interest rate and with it, our monthly payment.

Sitting in my office a few minutes later, I set the letter aside, took a deep breath and started typing. The avalanche of ideas that had come to me while I was watching Lizzy at Ken's had to go somewhere. Using an old technique, I wrote it in the form of an email to Vernon that I didn't intend to send. To make sure I didn't accidentally hit <Send> I used his nickname.

==========================
**Bill Crossley**
-------------------------------------------------
From: Bill.Crossley@syscon.com
To: The Vermin
Subject: Time Management - new approach

Vernon,

There is something strange and very wrong in expecting everyone to need the exact same collection of habits and practices in order to be effective. As professionals, we all have different wants and needs, depending on our industry, our training, the stage of our career and even the part of the world in which we happen to live. Professionals from Florida don't do things the way professionals from New York do. Our individual affinity for new gadgets and fancy software also plays an important role.

Improving our personal productivity and time management skills isn't about discovering the perfect set of practices once and holding on to them for the rest of our lives. Instead, improvement comes from making continuous changes, and our needs should drive those changes. It all starts with our decision to get better, something that never goes away for as long as we work for a living.

-----------------------------------------------

A nice start, I thought to myself. The soapbox was creaking under my weight. Better make sure I don't get carried away with the sound of my own voice.

"Our decision to get better." What did "better" mean, exactly? It usually meant more capable, but I began to see that it needed a new meaning. When my parents retired, they had actually made a conscious decision to handle less, which now appeared to me to be a kind of "downgrade" in terms of their time management skills. They had abandoned the practices they had used throughout their busy lives, settling into a much slower pace with fewer commitments.

By the same token, I needed better skills than my daughters did, because I had a lot more happening in my life that needed to get done. Lizzy only had to worry about a few classes at school, her homework, Karate, and playing on the swings. There was nothing wrong with how well she was managing the stuff in her life, and she didn't need the practices that I needed.

On a piece of paper, I wrote our names down.
Lizzy
Bill
Sandy, Mom, Dad

Who was missing from the picture? Someone in their early twenties, I decided. A young engineer hired straight from college who had just joined Syscon with its intense demands. Depending on their schooling, they could find the transition tough. For example, my struggles as an eighteen-year-old to adjust to Rutgers' engineering program probably led to the ease with which I slid into corporate life. In the office, Kumar Harbajan was the last of our new hires.

I added "Kumar" to the list, right under Lizzy. Beside each person, I decided to play around a bit. I added a Belt that showed a different level of skill.

Lizzy - White Belt
Kumar - Yellow Belt

Bill - Orange Belt
Mom, Dad - Yellow Belt (used to be Orange)

But these transitions happened in life all the time. I was about to make one by moving to RingCORE. When we moved to Florida, I had another. Buying a BrainPhone was one that was related to using a new technology. When they implemented Microsoft Outlook at work to replace an outdated email program, that was another. Going from doing the job of one person to that of three people? *Hell yeah.*

Moving from one skill level to another involved a kind of personal evolution. To some degree, it was driven by the sheer volume of demands in my life at any point in time. I remembered very clearly the craziness that Sandy and I went through when Lizzy was born. All of a sudden, we were short of time everywhere.

These turning points were a part of everyone's life.

What would Vernon say to all this? From the MTM point of view, everyone needed the same thing, all the time, forever. The book didn't quite say that, but it meant it. When I read it for the first time back in 1999, I liked that part, because it made me feel like I was discovering a final answer, or a secret that few others knew.

Now, the secret I was finding out was that there was no secret. Each person needed a customized, individual way to manage time.

But what about those people who had read Kripanali's book or attended one of his programs? What happened to them?

Well, the facts were right in front of me. Each of the members of the DAPE team had read most of the book and they were implementing bits and pieces, here and there, in a random, disorganized way. Would we ever be perfect followers?

Probably not... not with this crew. Not with any crew, maybe.

Wouldn't most people do what I did – use some stuff from MTM, pick up new stuff from other places, and keep moving?

Implementing MTM wasn't like plugging a USB device into a laptop. Human behaviour doesn't work like that.

Turning to Google, I searched phrases like "behavior change," "teaching habits" and then "adult learning." The stuff that came up blew me away.

Only nineteen percent of smokers diagnosed with lung disease were able to quit their smoking habits within a couple of years. As a non-smoker, I couldn't understand this, but I believed it. Even with motivation, changing habits is difficult. Going from a White Belt to a Yellow Belt took Lizzy three days a week at Ken's as well as practice sessions at home.

I tried writing all this down in my fake email and came up with something that was unfit for public consumption but helped me organize my thoughts. Leaning back in my seat, I felt spent as I stared out the window. There was a little snow on the ground, but the day was sunny and crisp. How many people out there had Vernons breathing down their necks, trying to get them to do impractical and impossible things?

But something felt right about the stuff I came up with, as I made a quiet decision. This was the last time I'd let someone else distract me with their ideas about my productivity. From now on, the best system to follow would be my own, as it always has.

Not that I'd try to become the next Xavier Kripanali. I wasn't about to go around writing books and teaching seminars. But I would be following my own set of habits and I'd focus my efforts on getting good ideas wherever I could.

Maybe I could use the time away from Syscon to build my system in some way. If the guys at RingCORE were productivity nuts, I might get some help with my time management skills and return to Syscon better than when I left. Now I felt ready to start work at RingCORE.

# Chapter 8

On the short drive over to RingCORE on a cold January morning, I was shivering. Part of it had to do with the cold snap we were having, but part was an unfamiliar, edgy feeling of expectation. Fortunately, I left early, so there was no need to rush as I mentally summarized everything I knew about the company.

I had found even more people with deep-seated grouses about RingCORE. Apparently, the firm used to be twice its current size in terms of revenues and headcount. Today it had only 1,500 people, which made it a little bigger than Syscon. From what I could piece together, the folks hired in the 1990's helped make it wildly successful, but a sharp drop in gaming revenue had dealt it a major blow.

As they spiraled into trouble, they pushed their people hard, forcing them to work longer, harder hours in order to survive. When the layoffs eventually came during 2005, they simply assigned more work to fewer people. That was a familiar story. And, as many explained, it didn't work.

The memories of those tough times hadn't gone away: RingCORE's ex-employees complained incessantly about being pushed past reasonable limits, giving up holidays and weekends whenever the company needed them. There were stories about postponed weddings, rescheduled funerals and cancelled vacations. I didn't like the sound of this at all. *Out of the pot and into the fire?*

I drove up to the building and parked in a rather empty lot. Or, to be more accurate, there were a lot of unfilled parking spaces, harkening back to a time when the company was much bigger. It was a long, squat, modern-looking building that was obviously intended for several thousand people, not a mere 1500. After parking, I walked up the stairs leading up the glass exterior.

As I pushed open the huge swinging doors to enter the building, I looked up at the vast expanse in awe. This building could hold four or five Syscons in its interior. Lost in my gazing, I was sharply interrupted by someone who called my name from behind the security gate.

"Hey, Bill, over here." Mark Springer loped over with a bounce in his step and shook my hand firmly. "Remember me?"

He was more energetic than I remembered. Or maybe my change in circumstances made everything and everyone look different. If I had known that he'd end up being my boss on an outside assignment, I would have paid more attention.

"I'll be handling your orientation today and, as you know, you'll be on my team for the next year. It's great to have you here - we have been suffering without an expert in Zebon for over a year, and I appreciate your agreeing to come."

I nodded and smiled, but inside I felt like a fraud. Little did he know that I was on the edge of being laid off, and I wasn't entirely sure what motivated the Syscon management team to send me away. Was it because I was highly thought of, or because it was a first step towards easing me out? Or did they just want to find a way to get RingCORE to share their payroll? I couldn't tell.

Nevertheless, he was being grateful, which made me feel oddly valued. It had been a long, long time since I last felt that way at Syscon.

We made our way down a couple of corridors to his office, while my eyes swept the environment for clues as to what I was about to take on. This was already looking different, as I couldn't see cubicles anywhere. Each person either had a private or semi-private office with a door and walls that ran from floor to ceiling. It made things very quiet, unlike the frantic, noisy cubicles of Syscon.

They also didn't seem to believe in the open-door policy, as many of them were closed. Did they have something to learn from us?

Mike's office was neat, but clearly active with lots of family pictures and Gantt charts - the favorite tool of project managers. Everything was neatly arranged, and the charts made me think that he was busy, but not so busy that he didn't pay attention to his environment.

That priority seemed to extend to the way he dressed. He wore a fresh polo shirt and khakis, which seemed to be the corporate dress standard in the company. It was a bit more informal than Syscon, where polo shirts were saved for dress-down days. Even though he was more casually dressed, he still looked just as neat as his office did.

He handed me a folder marked "Orientation" at the top. Every minute of the day was laid out in a schedule. The first thing he covered was the purpose and vision of the firm, which weren't printed on the page.

It was comforting, as if RingCORE deliberately took the time to bring newcomers on board. Upon my return to work at Syscon after Florida, it had taken a week to find an office, two weeks to find a desk, and a month to be assigned a laptop.

After we went through the preliminaries, he took me around to meet some other members of his team. I was introduced as "The Zebon guy from Syscon," and most people responded with a knowing nod. After meeting 50 people in a couple hours, my mind was spinning. I didn't have a moment to think before we were grabbing lunch in their huge cafeteria. A short trip to the supply store and we were back at my office – an office with an actual door.

Mike took me to a couple of meetings that afternoon to help get my feet wet. Neither one had much to do with Zebon directly, so there wasn't much for the "new guy" to say. That was cool with me, as I wanted to see the lay of the land before jumping in with "expert" comments.

But one thing did stand out. By Syscon standards, the meetings were short and intense. They spent more time than I had ever seen before setting things up at the start of the meeting, but the conversations were brisk and to-the-point. It all reminded me of the chat I'd had with Mike at the Hilton, but he didn't say much in either meeting, preferring to sit quietly. People in the meetings seemed almost over-prepared, and each discussion had a clearly defined objective. It was weird, as if they were trying to minimize the time spent together. It wasn't because they hated being together - far from it - but everyone seemed to have a train to catch.

That felt quite foreign to me. The best-run meetings at Syscon did look something like this, but they only happened once or twice a year. Most other meetings were lazy, casual affairs marked by in-meeting jokes and after-meeting complaints.

At around 4 p.m., Mike dropped by my new office to close out my orientation day. Boxes were still on the floor as I finished arranging some of my favorite items that I'd brought over from Syscon.

"Can I tell you a few things that you might have to change to be effective at RingCORE?"

Stunned, I stammered jokingly, "Why? Am I already doing something wrong?"

But he was all business.

"Do you remember when we first met, and I told you about our practice of not interrupting conversations to check digital devices? Today, during the meetings you attended, I noticed that you checked your BrainPhone quite frequently. You may have noticed that no one else did so. That's something you'll have to change. It's a clear sign here to others that you aren't managing your time-related habits well and that your time management system is out of control."

I didn't exactly agree that it was "out of control," but I sat there dumbstruck. I had made some progress since we first met on limiting this practice, but obviously not enough to impress these RingCORE folks.

* * *

He might as well have slapped me in the face. Not even Martha was this direct in her feedback.

My breath was stuck somewhere deep in my chest, so all I could do was sit and wait to see what he'd say next. He must have seen a look of concern flash across my eyes.

"Sorry Bill, I forgot for a moment that you are new to RingCORE and probably not used to such direct feedback." He smiled sympathetically, and I could feel cool air pull back into my lungs.

"Take a deep breath, buddy." We both laughed a sigh of relief. Or maybe he was just tickled.

"We probably do things quite a bit differently than you're used to."

I nodded, but still waited to see where he was going.

"You probably know that RingCORE almost went bankrupt about ten years ago. Part of what helped us survive the downturn was a number of "intense practices" that we implemented - Andre Anderson, our CEO, was the champion. 'We call them 'standices,' which is short for 'standard practices.' Andre did a number of experiments in personal productivity, and he focused on meetings. One of them was to start a meeting with the Purpose/Agenda/Logistics - PAL - framework, which I believe you have already seen?"

"Yes, I noticed it in the meetings this afternoon. You also used it with me back at the Hilton."

"Right. The one I just used with you is a standice for giving feedback: Observation/Impact/Suggestion. We didn't invent these, by the way, but Andre made them companywide standices after testing them out himself."

"Keep going," I said, as I started capturing these points in my BrainPhone.

"Make an Observation, Describe the Impact of the Behavior and Make a Suggested Change." I typed it all in; it sounded like stuff I already knew, but never really used.

"Anyone can make a change to a standice, or offer a brand new one. They start by conducting a few experiments themselves or with their team, and if it's shown to work, we accept it. Somewhere, someone is keeping a list of them, but by and large they are passed on in teachable moments like this."

I sat enthralled, loving what I was hearing. Learning and more learning. I loved it. Plus, the new terms were intriguing.

He explained, "We try to never get to the point where we are stuck in an unproductive way of working with each other. Looking back at the downturn, we see that getting stuck was one of the causes, even though the economy was also part of it. Long after the fact, we learned that several team members picked up some early warnings, but never said anything in the right meetings, due to poor meeting management."

He looked off in the distance for a moment. "I lost a lot of good friends. A lot." His voice was strained, and his gaze, which had been steady and strong until now, faltered as he paused to absorb a feeling that took him over for a few seconds before fading away. He shook his head.

"We just never want to go through that again. It's not just me – most of the old-timers feel the same way. My job is to make sure that the capacity of my time keeps expanding."

"So that you never get stuck again." Now, I wasn't just repeating his words, but referring to the notes I had taken after my revelation at Ken's Karate School.

"Never." The tone of finality in his voice gave me a shiver. Life didn't quite work out that way.

When he continued, he explained that smartphone abuse had spurred the most recent innovation in company policy. The company had been an early adapter of this new technology, so it wasn't long before everyone was happily multitasking and adopting some of the most extreme behaviors I'd ever heard of.

"We had meetings that went on forever, because people were doing everything else except minimizing the time while maximizing its value. Then, about three years ago, I was on a conference call with a manager, Daryll Chung, as he drove through a snowstorm near Binghamton. He was returning to Queens after visiting his son at Syracuse, but he kept driving through the storm without telling us that the snow had started. We were in the middle of a heated conversation about hiring more staff when he took a short break to send us all some data from his smartphone. When we tried to get him back, his phone went straight to voicemail. They found his body a day later at the bottom of a ravine."

He blinked hard.

"That was the end of our love affair with smartphones and all those tricky little things we do to cut corners. We realized after the fact that our intensity can get us in trouble if it's applied in unproductive or unsafe ways."

I nodded. This made so much sense, but it was too bad that I had to learn all this the hard way - by screwing up on the first day at work.

"I got it -- so no smartphones in meetings, or in conversations, and no multitasking."

I felt a little dumb, but I loved that I was learning just as I'd loved my school days. I always hated being tested against arbitrary criteria, but I loved learning new things and being excited to try them out for myself.

But then I remembered, "You said more than that earlier... something about my 'time-related habits'? What did you mean by that?" Based on the conversation so far, I needed to make sure that I made the most of every scrap of feedback at RingCORE. He paused and responded, "That's something new."

* * *

I stared, waiting for him to continue. Where was this going? Had he seen something about me that couldn't be fixed? Was it bad? How bad? Would it get back to Martha?

"One of our recent experiments looks at the way we manage ourselves and our productivity as individual professionals. It's the stuff that we usually call time management... except that it's actually about self-management; time can't be managed, as I'm sure you know."

"Sure." *Everyone knows this*, I pretended, so I nodded in agreement. It was a first for me, but this didn't seem like the right moment to appear clueless.

"We had tons of trouble operating effectively after the layoffs. The workload was the same, but now we had fewer people. Of course, our expectations of each other remained the same: ultra-high. People tried to keep up by simply working longer hours; initially, we all thought that smartphones would help. We believed that working and being available more would mean greater productivity."

I confirmed what he said with a smile. Hopefully, the three jobs I'd held at Syscon were being replaced by a single job at RingCORE. Also, my crusade to end my bad BrainPhone habits was in full launch mode.

"What we learned from trial and error was that each person needed an upgrade. Like, we were five years overdue. G taught us that each person needs a unique method in order to be most productive."

"G -- do you mean Graham Riley? The guy with the blog and the white papers?"

"Oh, good. Not too many people have heard of him. Andre fell in love with his thinking about unique methods, then shared his stuff around the company."

Intrigued, I leaned forward. Was this heading in the same direction as my own thoughts at Ken's?

At that moment, my BP chirped and then vibrated. I couldn't remember what that meant... was it a call, a text, a voice-mail? It distracted me for just a moment, and I actively decided to ignore it. My hand twitched, filled with the old habit of interrupting myself, but I stopped my fingers just before they reached the black BP holster at my hip.

"Are you saying that one size doesn't fit all? We each have different needs based on the number of commitments we have in life and the technologies that we prefer? And that we need to adjust our systems to match the things we deal with each day? And that time management books assume that we enter the class like kids, who don't know anything, when in fact we are adults who already have something in place?"

I must have sounded like Lizzy with my excitement.

He looked startled. "Have you been playing possum with me? You already know G's stuff!"

---

"A little, but not on this point. His site helped me think through my choice of using a schedule instead of a bunch of lists back in the fall. Since then, I have been thinking about this stuff non-stop."

"Really?" he said with more than a hint of curiosity.

Then my BP rang out aloud, and before I could stop myself, I whipped it out and stared at the screen to see who was calling. "Vernon Vaz." Didn't he get the memo? I shook my head, then noticed an email from Sandy asking how the day was going. I was just about to send her a quick reply when Mike tapped me on the arm with a look of honest pity.

Without even realizing it, I'd gone and done it again.

* * *

I quietly put away my BP, feeling simply awful. I felt like an addict.

"We had the same smartphone problem right here at RingCORE," he said with a hint of pathos in his voice. "I know that BrainCo -- the guys who make BP -- didn't intend to produce an addictive device that would end up costing productivity and endangering lives. We customers added that part."

"Mmm-hmm," I agreed, unsure of what to say next. Better to leave him thinking I was stupid rather than to say something to confirm it.

"What we learned is that we were all desperately trying to save time and increase efficiency, but we were doing it in ways that don't work. We were hoping that technology would solve our time management problems, as I bet you did when you got your BrainPhone."

He had no idea. Or did he?

"No need to feel bad. Everyone does it. We make these mistakes because we don't understand that our systems are made up of the time-related habits that I mentioned before. What we really should do is to get an understanding of our current way of managing time and think about the best way to improve it before even thinking about visiting Amazon or the Apple Store to buy the latest device."

I listened carefully, because he was applying some commonsense thinking to an area of life where none seemed to exist.

"Instead, we buy the device, then develop strange habits after the fact. All unconsciously and unthinkingly. It's putting the cart before the horse."

"Yeah!" I was impressed. Where did this stuff come from? How long did it take them to come up with this? Did they think about everything related to productivity with this much depth? Was there something in what he was saying that could save my job back at Syscon?

"But all this flies in the face of what time management gurus like Xavier Kripanali have been saying." Desperate to save face, I tried to show him that I did know a thing or two about time management.

"Oh yeah, MTM." He reached behind, plucking a well-worn copy from the shelf. "These books are pretty good, but they go overboard; they're too prescriptive. Lots of people here have read this and used bits and pieces -- like everyone else. No one at RingCORE tries to copy MTM's system in its entirety, or any other system for that matter. Not anymore. Instead, we use the stuff in books like MTM to modify our time-related habits. There are usually some good ideas, and we lift those out."

"You are singing my music," I said, nodding vigorously. "But what about his suggestions for scheduling? My most recent problem was that when I moved to Florida, I gave up all those lists and switched to scheduling everything. Recently, I tried to switch back to fit the book, but things only got worse. All sorts of tasks started falling through the cracks, and I just couldn't make it work for me the way it did ten years ago."

"Well, let's step back a bit. All of us use time-related habits to process the stuff we have to do each day. We read our email, make lists, arrange calendars, check Facebook… everything. By the time we get out of college and into our first jobs, we have something in place – it works for us that helps us get by. At that point, we haven't taken a class or read a book. This ad-hoc, self-taught approach is the norm, but some people fail because they don't teach themselves good techniques."

"Like Harry Henderson. He sat behind me in high school and ended up barely graduating because he never could find the time to study. College seemed like an impossible dream to him, so he never went."

"Right, exactly. Somewhere in our mid-thirties, working people like you and I pick up a book like MTM, which ignores what we have in place and tells us that there's one system of habits and practices we should follow." He paused before concluding loudly, "That's just plain wrong."

Now, he was emphatic, and I became very quiet.

"Xavier makes it worse by claiming that no one can replace his mandate of multiple to-do lists. But people here do it all the time. Especially project managers, who are crazy advocates of everyone using a schedule and carrying it around all the time. Xavier goes too far in taking a system that works for him, saying that we should all use it —if we don't, we're unproductive. The truth is, the research doesn't support everything he prescribes. It's a good system, don't get me wrong, but it doesn't fit everyone."

He stared at me to see what I had to say. For all he knew, I might be another letter-of-the-law disciple, like Vernon.

"Agreed in full," I exhaled loudly. "Thank you!"

He grinned, looking relieved. "It sounds as if you have been thinking about this kind of stuff for some time, too. That's great. We need more people to push the boundaries around here, as it's one thing that sets us apart from other companies. Maybe you could sit in on our Individual Productivity Council at some point? It's a structured brainstorm that we do every two weeks to figure out ways for our employees to be more productive. We try to focus more on underlying habits and principles rather than the gadget or tip of the month."

"Sign me up," I said without missing a beat. He quickly emailed me the Council's meeting schedule from his smartphone.

For the rest of the meeting, Mike went over the work I'd be doing as a member of his team. It wasn't rocket science. But I took careful notes, because I kept imagining what it would be like to be in a council meeting with some sharp cookies who were all interested in time management.

As he left my office, I grinned at no one in particular. *If this is what working here is like, then I think I can live with it.* My phone rang as I sat down.

Vernon.

\* \* \*

I stood up as I answered the phone.

"Hello, Vernon," I said, greeting him by name.

"Bill, our meeting is in about a half hour. Where are you?"

"Didn't you get my email from last week? My assignment at RingCORE started today, so I'm at my new office in their building."

"Oh, I guess I need to catch up on my email. That's not supposed to happen, dammit." He sounded annoyed.

"It was in that email with the requirements for the software we want to purchase." He needed that information for the meeting, I remembered.

"Hold on, Bill, I'm getting another call." Before I could protest, he put me on hold, which I hated. Why didn't he just let it roll over to voicemail?

After five minutes that felt like 20, I heard, "Bill, are you there? You need to do a better job of breaking up your emails into smaller messages. People have a hard time getting through your emails because they have too much in them."

I went from a simmer to a boil.

"How is your MTM implementation coming along? Have you gotten your lists straightened out? You should be fully compliant by now."

Deep breath. Squaring my shoulders I announced slowly, "I'm not using MTM any longer."

"You can't do that!" he sputtered, almost shouting in my ear. "You'll fail. You need to do better, or else you'll deserve to be..." His voice trailed off. "You won't succeed this way." Now, his voice was icy.

My heart skipped a beat, but I was standing in a RingCORE office, fresh from a great conversation with Mike, and I had a Productivity Council meeting in my calendar.

"Deserve to get what, Vernon? I'm not using MTM because it doesn't work for me; my own system does. It's a waste of time and effort to try to follow something from a book when I have been using a better alternative. So, no. I will be more productive, but not by going back to MTM. I'm back to doing my own thing, and it's already an improvement."

That last part was a bit of an exaggeration, I admit.

"You can't do that" he repeated. "Xavier Kripanali clearly states that his system is—" but I cut him off.

"Vernon, what Xavier has to say is just an opinion based on his individual experience. There's no reason to think that his system should work for me any more than my system should work for him."

"Okay, you know what? Whatever. It's your life to screw up." With that passing shot, my BrainPhone fell silent.

# Chapter 9

The next few weeks were a struggle as I tried to match the intensity of my new colleagues. I ended each day the same way - feeling tired to the bone.

True, I left the office shortly after 5 p.m. every day, just like everyone else. That meant that I could spend more time with Sandy and the kids, in theory. Unfortunately, by the time I got home in the afternoons, I had only enough energy to say hello before I collapsed into my easy chair for an instant nap.

"Stressful day?" Sandy asked after seeing me repeat this routine every day for a week.

"Not really." I paused to shake the cobwebs out of my head after finishing up that day's nap a few minutes earlier. "Not stressful like I don't like it, or wish it would go away. More like.... intense. I have to change gears to keep up with these people. Plus, there is so much to learn. Not about Zebon, but they do things so differently -- there's not a moment wasted in this place."

"Does everyone collapse after going home? Or is that because you're new?"

"They do the normal stuff -- they have a basketball team and go bowling. I think it's because I am taking it all in so quickly. It's like a hard sprint each day."

But as I explained to Martha in an email the following week, I was truly enjoying the experience. Yes, the technical side of things was interesting; I was able to apply the Zebon technology in a way that was innovative and original. I was even more captivated by the RingCORE way of getting things done.

Their expectation was clear - I should be able to pick their standices up quickly. Mike got all the other members of the Ohara Project team to help me, which they did in their own ways. With constant corrections, my smartphone habits shifted considerably. It was hard to continue in the same old way when everyone was watching and giving feedback, but I never once felt attacked by any of it.

They were super smart; any one of my new colleagues would stand out from the crowd at Syscon.

I learned another clue to their productivity when I sat down to lunch with Mike on Wednesday during my sixth week at RingCORE.

"Have you read the book *Flow*?"

"No -- but that's a term you guys keep using. What's it about?"

"It's written by a guy with a name that's impossible to pronounce, but it's all about creating the conditions for peak performance, particularly at work. We combined that stuff with some research done on software programmer productivity in the "Code Wars" of the 1990's. They both concluded similar things." He Googled the book and the author for me, "Mihaly Csikszentmihalyi."

"What similar things did they say?" I asked.

"One key component to being productive involves getting the necessary space, time and quiet in order to do your best work. When you have it, you can work for hours without feeling tired and still be creative and innovative. It's sometimes even ecstatic, particularly when you're making progress and the task is challenging, but not ridiculously impossible. We call it the 'flow state' here at RingCORE, and once you get in it, you don't want it to end."

"At Syscon, we called that 'staying at home to get some real work done'." That got a laugh. "Seriously -- if you wanted to get serious work done, you had to abandon your cubicle... or even the entire building." I told him about the way engineers would call in sick in order to meet a deliverable by working at home. The joke became that "Syscon was no place to get work done."

"I'm more used to the always-busy feeling of jumping from one thing to another -- following one interruption after another. It's called 'being responsive'."

"You have probably noticed that we hate to be interrupted?"

"Tell me about it," I answered. "The other day, I interrupted the guy in the office next door to mine and he almost bit my head off. He only gave me a break because he realized I was new. I thought the sign on his door was a joke: I'M BUSY."

"Never interrupt a RingCORE employee in the flow state," Mike said, laughing. "But seriously, it's one of the keys to our success, so you should probably check out the book. *Peopleware* by DeMarco and Lister -- the Code War guys -- is also interesting."

Within the hour, both eBooks whizzed to my laptop and BrainPhone.

*  *  *

Back in my office, I couldn't wait to read both books, so I downloaded a two-page summary of *Flow* and *Peopleware* to get the abbreviated versions. I quickly learned that it took more than 20 to 30 minutes to return to the "flow state" after being interrupted, so it was important to guard oneself against unnecessary stops, no matter how enticing, friendly, or automatic they might be.

In the next week, I watched RingCORE people closely as I read both books. They obviously took this stuff to heart, making me realize why they seemed to have their smartphones under control. Turning off most alerts, they carefully managed their ringers, beeps and buzzes, switching them on and off several times per day, depending on circumstances.

Their practices all helped make meetings and conversations more intense. My hand, by contrast, couldn't get rid of what a few jokingly called my "BrainPhone Itch." When I joined them and turned off my notifications, I felt like something had been taken away. I instantly missed the little distractions in the middle of tense discussions, for example. My mini-vacations during meetings were also a thing of the past.

The other big change for me was to follow the popular RingCORE practice of altering my Microsoft Outlook settings. At Syscon, we just accepted the program's defaults with its visible pop-ups and little dings that came onto the screen when email arrived.

At RingCORE, I learned that you could turn these off and control the flow of email using the auto-download switches. Even my BrainPhone had a similar setting.

Checking email became an entirely different experience, and the Zero Inbox, which I had struggled to accomplish at Syscon, became a daily reality. My Tzinbox score rose steadily. It was different – I wasn't compulsively checking messages all the time, and I wasn't jumping from one unproductive state to the next.

I also noticed that they were very focused on something they called "the difference," which reminded me of what Sandy had been reading about lately. Their use of this strange lingo seemed connected to some blend of making a contribution of some kind, stirring things up, and making future results happen. Before long, I took to the phrase as my own and started using it in meetings, just like everyone else. We used it to center discussions and pull them away from trivia.

Of course, Sandy noticed these shifts in behavior.

"It's weird... you take a nap every day when you get back from the office, but you haven't done much work at home since you started at RingCORE." We were chatting on the verandah during an unusually warm Friday evening in spring. We spoke while watching Lizzy play on the swings with a neighbor from next door and Rebecca take some tentative baby steps.

"No, I haven't... and I don't miss it one bit. I like having the choice. The downside is that the work is tougher and more draining. I have to use every single muscle in my body to cope with the sheer volume of work that needs to be done. It's the hardest I have ever worked, yet I feel like I'm just barely keeping up."

"How about everyone else?" she asked, concerned. "How do they cope?"

"They don't seem to have a problem. It's those of us who are new to the company who are having a hard time. I met a couple of other newbies, and they're also running pretty ragged. It takes some getting used to; it's not easy to have to stretch so fast and so hard in order to play your part. While they expect you to manage your own productivity, they don't exactly give you much training."

"By the way, Honey, not to change topics all of a sudden, but have you paid the Visa and Amex bills?"

My heart sank. Back in my Syscon days, I used to carry bills with me to the office, but now I had no time to look at them at work; I hadn't gotten used to the idea of doing them at home. The result was predictable... they were now late.

She could tell what had happened by my non-answer.

Without further comment, she continued. "Your parents are saying that they never get to see us anymore, and they are going to need some of your help with the yard. Also, don't forget that we have the dentist's appointments next week and doctor's appointments the week after."

Although she went on adding stuff to my already burdened to-do list, I don't remember what else she said. I tuned out after the word "doctor" because it all seemed like too much. My mind drifted away to the plans for the weekend, which I hoped would involve lots of time doing absolutely nothing. I needed to recuperate after a hard week.

"Bill!' she screamed. Over at the swing set, Lizzy was lying face down with her hand in the air, crying out. Behind her was a broken swing dangling from the chain.

---

We ran over and picked her up from the ground. She looked at both of us with startled eyes before breaking out in a grin. "I'm okay -- can I get a do-over?"

Thank God, nothing was wrong with her. Something was wrong with me, however, and Sandy shot me a stern look. A week earlier, she had asked me to fix the swing after seeing it coming loose. I hadn't gotten around to it.

"Be as good at home as you are at work, and we'll get along just fine," she hissed angrily. As she took a shaken Lizzy inside, I stood staring at the broken swing set. *How the hell do I keep track of all the small things?*

* * *

Ten days later, I was still stinging from Sandy's angry comments. We made up later that day, but I couldn't escape her logic. She was right.

How was I going to take the next step to manage all aspects of my life? Something was confusing about the way I looked at the way the world came at me each day. It was flying in so quickly, from so many angles that I didn't have a way to keep on top of everything. I was convinced that I had more stuff to do than ever before. RingCORE's intensity made sure of that.

Or was it information overload? Perhaps there was just too much stuff available for us to read, browse, watch and listen to in this day and age? A television show I watched proudly proclaimed that the average professional dealt with more information in a day than their grandparents saw in a month.

Stuff. No... too much stuff. Why wasn't I able to handle it all more skillfully?

These thoughts were bubbling around in my head as I parked the car in RingCORE's lot and made my way inside. It was a little over two months after my arrival at the company, and on the way in that morning, I stopped to check email before heading to my first Productivity Council meeting.

Mike was already there with about ten other people from around the office I had not yet met. It looked like a cross-section of RingCORE, with an almost perfect mix of experience.

The meeting started on a topic that the previous session had left incomplete. They were talking about "electronic packets." I had heard this piece of RingCORE jargon bouncing around, but no one had ever defined it for me.

Mike took a moment to explain. "The term 'packet' comes from one of the company's founders, who picked it up from a steel mill construction project he'd worked on in the 1960's. Back then, work was divided into "packets." These were physical envelopes that carried documents; the documents outlined tasks for the recipient to accomplish. At the appropriate step in a project, packets were handed out to each member of the team who needed to perform a particular task."

Of course, paper packets were no longer handed out, but the term still held at RingCORE. The word had become degraded over the years so that it now included casual email messages, assignments in meetings and even tasks arising from informal conversations.

Some members of the team wanted to bring it back. One older guy with a long grey beard made the point, "Where I used to work in the eighties, we had packets, too, and everyone knew exactly what they were doing. None of the nonsense we have today with stuff flying all over the place. Back then, you knew exactly what you needed to do and when it was due. Paper worked fine for us then and we can make it work again. It would give us some control over the stuff that ends up disappearing through the cracks."

There were groans around the room. No one was a fan of that idea, apparently, and someone joked about "killing more trees to make packets."

Mike chimed in, "I hate the word 'stuff.' Packet sounds so much clearer and crisper. Maybe we don't need paper, but we need the right way to talk about work."

The conversation continued back and forth for a few minutes but seemed to be going nowhere. During a lull in the discussion, I asked, "When packets were around, were the recipients obliged to accept them in full?"

This spurred a bout of disagreement, but a consensus arose that there was usually some kind of negotiation to arrive at an agreed plan of work. In all cases, the person receiving the packet had the final say.

"So the packet itself wasn't the most important thing; it was actually the decision that the person made about what they were going to do?"

"Where are you going with this, Bill?" asked Grey Beard. I couldn't recall his name.

I wasn't sure, to be honest, but I responded anyway. "It doesn't seem as if the magic was in the packet, but in the decision. The packet only helped make it clear exactly what the individual was agreeing to. If that's the case, then we don't need better packets, but better agreements."

"Are you suggesting that we negotiate every deliverable?" asked Grey Beard.

"No, but something happens during the process of a negotiation -- a commitment gets made. Today, we are still making commitments, except that we don't have time to negotiate them." Now, everyone was listening. With the spotlight on me, my heart started to beat a bit more quickly and I could feel my mouth going dry.

"I am imagining something like a 'personal packet' that we create when we decide to do something in the future, whether anyone else knows about it or not. In the old days, the paper document in an envelope triggered the creation of a personal packet, but in today's world, it all happens in our minds."

"Is it the same task as the one outlined in the envelope?" asked someone.

"It may be, but not necessarily. Just because you are asked to do something, doesn't mean that you create a personal packet... a commitment to do it."

"But what are you agreeing to?" someone else asked.

"Some kind of outward commitment based on your own internal decision." My answer was fuzzy, but my mind was becoming clearer.

"A personal packet is a decision that you make to do something in the future. While its creation can be prompted by an email, a request, a document or conversation, the outcome is always the same. It gets created in the mind. You might share it with others, but that's not a requirement."

Mike continued the thought, "When I look at a Gantt chart or a plan for a new project, I know that I instantly create a bunch of personal packets."

"Right. And each personal packet carries with it a duration and a start or end time."

I paused, looking for a reaction, but there was only a thoughtful silence. I felt the need for someone else to jump in, as I really didn't know where this would end up. Looking around the room, I tried to spur someone else to pick up the baton, but no one seemed ready.

I continued, "If I look at the same Gantt chart that Mike described, but I'm not involved in the project at all, then it's likely that I'll create no personal packets. Just because I'm exposed to certain information, requests for action, invitations, data, websites, blogs, whatever.... that doesn't mean that I'll create a personal packet. Once I do, however, things change."

An older guy piped up, "When I studied factory engineering, we used to focus on widgets. A widget is just just a generic term used for anything that's being made in factory, or being included in a larger assembly. Maybe this personal packet is like a widget. Nothing happens in a factory until a widget starts moving down an assembly line. Maybe nothing happens in a project until a team member creates a personal packet."

Now, heads were nodding around the room.

Mike added, "Because it's a mental creation, you can't touch it. I think that when you complete the actions defined by a personal packet, it just disappears. Like our commitment to finish this meeting on time. When we all walk out of this room... that commitment disappears, as if it never existed."

More nods.

A young lady with a very serious face said, "Wouldn't too many personal packets cause stress? I agree with Mike that they are mental, but that doesn't mean they aren't real in some way. Sleepless nights come from having too many. People quit when they think they have too many packets to handle and feel overburdened."

Grey Beard added, "When people get stressed or they can't manage their personal packets, a bunch of them don't get completed on time. They get labeled by other people as poor time managers."

Immediately, my mind flashed to the broken swing set, Lizzy and the bills. All Sandy saw was a bunch of my packets falling by the wayside.

Mike got excited and asked "Is that what time management really means? Creating and moving around personal packets until the action is done, and then they disappear? It's impossible to manage time, but you certainly can manage these personal packets. Maybe we need to stop talking about the vague 'stuff' we have to do and move to discuss personal packets instead?"

There were groans and sighs. The term was too clunky and it was hard to see it working. "We'll bite our tongues off trying to talk about simple stuff." That got a laugh as people played with the term "personal packet" and put it into sentences starting with the letter p, "Peter Pringle picked a personal packet promoting Personnel's project past performance perfectly..."

After a few minutes, we threw out the term "personal packet" and agreed to use the term "time demand."

And all of a sudden, just like that, I could see time demands everywhere.

* * *

I once heard an old proverb.

An old fish swims past two young fish. As he greets them, he says, "How about that water today? It's really something isn't it?" The two young fish smile and nod politely, but a few seconds after swimming away, one looks at the other and asks, "What's water?"

I felt like a young fish who had just learned to see water. It was as if someone turned on a switch, and suddenly, time demands were everywhere. The days immediately following the Productivity Council were the most startling. I could see them sprouting up everywhere: in meetings on the Ohara project, in casual conversations with Sandy, while reading a novel on my Kindle and during sleep when I had a problem at work to solve. My mind seemed to be a 24-7 factory for these little buggers.

When Lizzy asked me to take her to a Karate lesson the following week, or Sandy reminded me to pay a bill, I created time demands. As I drove home from work listening to an advertisement on a radio station and decided to visit the local computer store to take advantage of a sale, I created one more. These little personal commitments were invisible and intangible, but they had psychological weight that felt quite real. My direct experience matched the findings of the meeting perfectly.

There were times when I wouldn't record a new time demand, thinking that I could remember it later. Sometimes I did recall it, but sometimes I didn't. That inconsistency created problems, as some time demands simply slipped through the cracks. Others would stay around for a while before disappearing from my memory.

I noticed that some were harder to pick out than others. When I wanted to make a decision but hadn't thought about it enough, I didn't realize at first that the time demand was "to think about the problem until I got somewhere." I learned that distinguishing my actual, precise commitment wasn't easy.

A new energy surged through me as I went about my daily activity. As the next Council meeting approached, I prepared for it excitedly, tingling inside.

Due to some conflicts in the schedule, the next Productivity Council meeting was held only a few weeks later. I presented a summary of what we had discovered during the prior meeting and what I had done with it since then. I flashed up the following definition of a time demand in a series of Power Point slides:

TIME DEMANDS are individual commitments to complete single actions in the future.
 - They are created by the individual's mind.
 - Their creation might be prompted by any triggering event.
 - They accumulate in the mind.
 - They disappear once the action has been completed.
 - Personal memory is a dangerous place to store a time demand.
 - Time demands can be "moved" from one place to another (e.g. from email message to list).
 - They can be shared, to some degree, between people.
 - They are the "atoms" of time management, even though they are psychological, not physical, objects.
 - An email Inbox is an example of a passive or automatic collector of time demands.
 - A paper pad is an example of an active or manual collector of time demands.
 - Poor time managers lose track of time demands and end up not completing them.

I explained to the team, "In all the time management books and programs I looked at, I couldn't find anything similar. We have found a missing link that could help RingCORE." When I concluded, I said "I think that if we help people focus on the right "widget," we will help them manage their efforts to become more productive."

The short silence after my call for questions made me wonder if this would be my last Productivity Council meeting. They were studying the last slide when, all of a sudden, the room broke into applause. I was surprised, to say the least.

Mike even started whooping as if he were at a football game cheering an interception. I shook my head in disbelief. It looked as if this might be something important, after all.

"This is the start of something big." announced Grey Beard. Someone else asked, "Now that we have gotten somewhere, what can we do with this?" A number of questions and answers started flying back and forth, and I desperately tried to capture them all while dropping in my own opinion here and there.

The big question was, "How does this definition translate into greater productivity?" I didn't have a ready answer other than "notice them when you see them." Some had ideas about time demands ending up in schedules, lists or in other storage areas like address books, or password apps. Others wondered if they truly disappeared, or just gave birth to new time demands, making life more complex. Someone wanted to simulate the flow of time demands throughout a professional's life to see what different approaches might yield. It was a rich discussion that we cut short because another group was waiting outside to use our room. As we filed out talking with each other, we were still buzzing.

Mike stopped me in the hallway outside the meeting room as I tried to prolong the feeling of being in the flow state by answering all the questions that anyone had. He said, "I don't know how you do it -- a great presentation like that even with the one you have to do tomorrow. Good job."

And then it came back to me. Three weeks ago, I had promised to give a presentation on the Zebon technology to a group of senior managers led by Mike, so they could evaluate its potential for use in a new project. It completely fell off my radar. I smiled and said, "Don't worry about that -- it's all taken care of!"

He laughed and I hoped that my momentary frantic look had been lost on him. The truth was that I'd have to zip back to my office to get a start on it. Plus, I faced a tough explanation to Sandy. My Dad had been feeling under the weather lately and we were planning to take the kids over to see him tonight. My parents were looking forward to seeing us, and now I was forced to disappoint everyone.

So much for the victorious discovery of time demands. It obviously wasn't enough.

# Chapter 10

Back in my office scrambling to get tomorrow's presentation together, I had a bitter taste of defeat. I thought I had gotten somewhere. Just moments before Mike's reminder, it felt as if the heavens had opened up, and I had finally accomplished something.

But over here on the ground, this new idea hadn't done a thing for me, except provide a name for the stuff that was now falling freely through the cracks.

*Some accomplishment.*

My sarcasm didn't hide the fact. There was still a big hole remaining in my methods.

Putting these thoughts aside, I entered the flow state and focused my attention on crafting the presentation in PowerPoint. After two hours of effort, I ended up by adding a few final touches to slides that, for the most part, were borrowed from prior decks. It was almost 8 p.m.

I remained haunted by this, my latest failure, all the way until it was time to go to bed. Instead, I padded into my office and clicked on the computer monitor.

I searched YouTube for some clips on manufacturing, pulling up an interview with a manager at an auto plant. An engineer, he explained how small parts were made from hunks of rubber, glass, steel, fabric, fiber-glass and metal by being pulled and pushed in different ways until a car popped out at the end. In an auto plant, giant machines were used to shape parts by cutting, molding, heating, cooling, flattening, stamping... plus other actions. It looked miraculous.

If a time demand was like a widget, then similar forces must exist to act on it until the result was a real world action. That analogy seemed to work. What were these forces that acted on time demands? How did they get pushed one way and pulled another?

After surviving the presentation the following morning, I was stopped in the hallway by Mike. "I sent you email this morning with a link to some restricted stuff on G's website. Check it out when you have a moment."

Opening Mike's email, I found a password and started poking around. There was a lot of information, all of it good, but I started to see an answer to my question about these mysterious forces.

From his research base near Cornell, G had discovered some striking similarities in the way that people process their responsibilities each day. He didn't have a concept similar to "time demands" so he used words like "stuff," or "workload." According to him, humans used "temporal behavior patterns" to process the time-based stuff that comes into our lives. These were made up of a constellation of habits, practices and rituals that each person used to deal with time demands.

He showed that the patterns that all working people use could be aggregated and shown to be quite similar, no matter the person's location or background. All of us, he argued, are subject to the limits of our humanity and the laws of physics. There was an underlying structure to the actions we take to manage the stuff we do each day. His latest research showed that the books and programs on time management were all offering variations on a single theme. Understanding the underlying, unifying theme should allow for better skills, he reasoned, as well as better tools.

He got my attention with his example of smartphone abuse as a solid case of large numbers of people attempting to become more productive without knowledge of the underlying themes in time management. With some hilarious YouTube clips, he showed desperate people using ineffective methods to try to get better. Of course, I recognized almost all of them from personal experience. "I was making good progress cutting most of them out," I thought.

According to G, people used six foundation actions to manipulate email messages: Arriving, Deciding, Deleting, Completing Now, Keeping, and Listing.

The idea was very simple. Email comes into our Inboxes automatically - he called that "Arriving." We then make a decision about how to dispense with it ("Deciding"), and at that point we have 4 choices. We can Delete it, work on it immediately ("Completing Now,") place it in some kind of archive - (Keeping) - or add it to a To-Do list, which he called "Listing."

The words he used were interesting. These were the automatic ways we act on email messages, without thinking and without being taught. While most professionals never took an "email management" class, he explained that they all use variations of the same core steps. He seemed more intent on describing the current way that all professionals manipulate email than attempting to impose a new or ideal process.

However, when he compared the way people processed email, he found that many missed certain steps. When they taught themselves, they lacked an appreciation of the overall picture, which led to gaps. He gave the example of a user with 50,000 messages in an Inbox as one whose practices were clearly deficient.

Others ran into problems when their email volumes exceeded a certain threshold. All of a sudden, their habits started to fail them. This was exactly what had happened to me when Anna and Joe left, and I had received their workloads. My Tzinbox got worse, and didn't recover until I left for RingCORE.

G's idea was that we all lacked a way to see the flaws clearly: a working "philosophy." By and large, we were left to our own devices to try to work out our everyday problems, like getting too much email: a common complaint in every company that I knew of. G tried to make it clear that the problem was not the number of messages, but the fact that our self-taught systems were inadequate. That was interesting, but as I downloaded a fresh round of email, I didn't know whether all this had some practical value or was just nice theory.

Up popped a new message from Nick Holleran entitled, "Syscon Employee Productivity Study." As the company's CEO, he had commissioned some research on employee productivity. The consultants' report showed that there was a direct link between the company's recent losses and its "excessive headcount." Compared to other companies, we were on the low end of the scale in terms of output per employee. They singled out the Project Management level for particular attention, describing the project and time management skills being used as "in need of modernization." Overall, there was room to improve employee output by 23%.

What was left unsaid in the summary was whether or not that improvement would come from laying off staff or improving employee skills. But everyone knew which one was easier to implement. That program had already started.

*I'm so glad I'm not there.*

However, deep down, I knew there was no way to escape the impact of this study. Remembering how Anna got stranded in California, I decided to be careful about ensuring my return to Syscon, even though it was now only May.

* * *

A few days later, I was sitting at my desk when G's latest newsletter appeared in my Inbox. It included a new article on the difficulty people experienced in their efforts to change entrenched behavior.

He wrote, "Though people often make decision to change their time management practices, why do so many of them fail?" He gave the example of heart attack victims. After six months, more than half hadn't cut back on their fast food habits. That led him to believe that it was much harder to change time management habits than he had realized.

It was such an intriguing article that I lost track of time - deep in the flow state once again. Rushing off to my next meeting, I arrived five minutes late with my head still lost in those new ideas.

Fifteen minutes later, someone mentioned the Ohara project, and my mind snapped back to the meeting. I answered a few questions about the Zebon technology, trying my best not to be distracted. Half an hour later, as we started to leave, Andre Anderson walked in. This was my first time meeting him close up, so I sat up just a bit.

He greeted everyone and asked us to stay a few extra minutes in a slightly posh British accent. As we all sat down, he thanked us politely. "I really just want to get a sense of how we can use the stuff you are working on in the mid-term to get our revenues up. After all, the board is going to be hunting for my scalp if they don't see us going in the right direction."

This got a quick laugh, and our attention zeroed in on what he was about to say. He seemed like just a regular guy, even though his accent made me think of Princes and Duchesses.

He took a moment to introduce himself to the couple of us who were sitting in a meeting with him for the first time. Afterwards, he started sharing how the company was planning to use its new education thrust to "make a big difference." Gaming was profitable in the short term, but he predicted that the market would become saturated and eventually the principles of good game design would make their way into new markets. RingCORE was betting that education would be a big new opportunity.

"But I need more movement on that Zebon technology. It needs to be incorporated into our new offerings as soon as possible and I'm concerned that we're not moving fast enough." The room fell silent and he looked at me.

"Bill, what can you do to move things along?" The words were stuck in my throat - I wasn't prepared for his question. I stammered something about trying to use G's techniques to accelerate the project and he cut me off, "That stuff isn't ready for Prime Time yet. What else have you got?"

"We have been working on something called time demands - the equivalent of a factory widget, but in the world of time management. It's a commitment to complete an action in the future and our success comes down to our ability to manage them well. It might help us become more productive." It sounded lame, weak and flaky.

He stared at me with what I can only call a "You Idiot" expression. He paused long enough for all the energy in the room to evaporate, leaving me lifeless, while everyone else stalled like cars caught in a traffic jam.

He looked at his watch impatiently and said "I gotta go -- make time to see me tomorrow. Call my secretary."

And then he left. More than a few eyes looked at me with pity, and I think someone even patted me on the shoulder. All I know is that within a few seconds every other person quickly followed Andre out of the room leaving me sitting alone.

* * *

In a daze, I made my way to my office. *What now? What had I done? What had I said?*

By the time I got back to my desk, Andre's secretary had already sent an email to set up a meeting for 8 a.m. He wanted to get this done quickly. *Why?* I wiped my palms on my pants, not caring about the sweat. Taking a deep gulp of air released a little of the tension built up by the short breaths I had started taking since my fun ride at RingCORE came to a screeching halt a few minutes earlier.

*What's the worst that could happen?*

A list started to form on a scrap of paper with the help of a blue pen.

1. *Back to Syscon*: This could mean the end of my career. Pissing off a CEO whom we were trying to partner with was a bad move.

2. *Scrap --> Zebon:* Perhaps Andre wanted to kill the new technology. If so, why didn't he just say so?

3. *Better performance on Zebon:* Maybe he wanted me out of the leadership role. To replace me with someone else.

Putting together and pulling apart these scenarios in my mind didn't help me feel any better. It just didn't look good.

But I needed to go into the meeting with something prepared. He was obviously focused on Zebon's progress; in today's meeting, he'd cut me off just as I started getting into time demands, so this meeting wouldn't be about that.

I stared at my clock on the wall. It was already 5 p.m., but I needed to pull some kind of presentation together in time for our 8 a.m. meeting tomorrow. If he wanted to know all about Zebon, I was going to be the one to tell him. I called home and told Sandy that "I'll be late... no, make that very late" for dinner. Yet again, she understood quickly that I was up against some kind of pressure and told me to "Just get home safely, Honey."

Scanning my email messages before starting, I noticed an announcement from Syscon. Anna's last conversation with me on the phone before she had gone for good flashed to my mind as my pulse came alive with a fresh pounding.

20 people gone. But I was safe. Jack. Cheng. Albertina. Plus a bunch of others from I.T., HR and Marketing - they were packing up their stuff.

*This is simply awful.* Sitting around waiting for your name to be called like this. It was no way to work, and I imagined that at Syscon, all work had effectively stopped for the week.

Nick's passing comments at the bottom of the announcement were cryptic. "It is expected that further right-sizing efforts will be undertaken in alignment with the results of the Employee Productivity Study." *What an asshole.*

Also in the batch of email was a message from Ted, forwarding the announcement to my personal email address. "Did you see this crud? We are okay, but now there's the same amount of work for fewer people, as usual. We cannot continue like this... like sitting ducks. We need to go down fighting, but what does that even mean? Talk about depressing. And I'm the most upbeat guy around here. Okay, also the most sarcastic. Sorry to remind you of this stuff - be careful over there. P.S. Your buddy Vernon is pretty bummed these days. Management finally came out and confirmed that there won't be any more promotions for a long time."

Shutting down my email, I opened up PowerPoint and pulled out some Zebon slides. Tomorrow, I'd be sinking or swimming, but I wouldn't be drowning without a fight.

* * *

The following morning, as I headed to the elevators to meet with Andre, I felt under-prepared, even though I was armed with a 50-page presentation outlining Zebon's progress.

It was entitled, "Zebon - Its History and Future." I packed it with lots of cool graphics and stock-photos of earnest, smiling middle-manager types, hoping they would help make the case that we were doing well enough to be left alone. Mike should be at this meeting, I grumbled. He was the Team Leader after all, and it didn't make sense for us to have a discussion without him there. "Who would answer the hard questions that I couldn't?" I asked myself warily.

I slipped into the elevator, so lost in my thoughts that I barely took note of a very quiet, older Black man who appeared to be in his 60's. He looked like he didn't belong here at RingCORE, as his outdated suit showed that he had cut his teeth in a bygone era and never quite caught up. *Maybe he's an ex-employee,* I guessed, as I seemed to remember his face and the company encouraged its retirees to stick around.

When the doors opened, I walked over to Andre's office and sat down in a little waiting area that was decorated like a scene from Mad Men, my second-favorite television show. Funnily enough, the retiree sat down in the waiting area also. We nodded at each other and he picked up a magazine. When Andre's administrative assistant beckoned him over, I heard him speak with a slight accent. It sounded Indian to me, but his features didn't quite match those of a person from the subcontinent.

A few minutes later, I was asked to join them.

"Bill, have you met Graham Riley? People around here call him 'G'."

I was stunned. Mike told me that there was some connection between the writer and RingCORE, but I was hardly expecting him to visit in person. Meeting someone whose work you have been studying in depth - well, that was a first, and it felt a little weird. Was I awestruck? Maybe.

*What in the world did he have to do with Zebon?*

"Pleased to meet you," I said with just a hint of a question in my voice. Andre must have picked up on it, as he hurriedly explained, "I would like to continue that conversation we started yesterday about time demands, but I wanted to see if we could put it to use. I knew that G was coming in today, so I thought we'd complete it today. Okay by you?"

I nodded and squeezed the thumb-drive in my pocket before letting it go.

My face must have looked as lost as I felt, because Andre joked to me, "Bet I had you guessing, huh?" I laughed nervously as all the tension built up over the last night dissipated. He turned to G and said "I didn't have time to brief Bill on the purpose of our meeting and why I wanted to connect you two. I guess I didn't brief you either, for that matter? The blind leading the lost!"

Now we were all laughing without reservation. A silly comment, but it did the trick and brought us together.

"Tell G what we were talking about in yesterday's meeting."

I mumbled again and blurted out "time demands."

Fumbling for words, I tried not to think about Andre having the power to end my career with a bad recommendation. They both looked at me with an expectation that made time stand still for just a few pulses. I felt the thoughts turn more fluidly into words.

"I guess it all started with us talking about how manufacturing engineers focus on widgets. The word is just a substitute for the materials and sub-assemblies that make their way from raw material to the end-product. In time management or personal productivity, there is no agreed-upon "widget"; instead, most people talk about 'stuff'." With that level of imprecision, however, we are left with only a vague idea of what exactly we need to work on."

Their gaze was intense, which fed my confidence.

"We defined a new term: a time demand. It's an individual commitment to undertake an action in the future." I went on to explain all the characteristics the team had defined in the meeting and emphasized, "It's a psychological object with some physical properties."

Their eyebrows shot up.

I felt emboldened. "When you don't know what a time demand is, you have little hope of improvement because you don't own up to your role as an originator." They were not just nodding, but were looking at each other as if they wanted to jump in, but they motioned for me to keep going.   .

"We cannot escape the fact that our minds work this way. The only question is, what do we do with these suckers once they come into existence in our heads? That's when I came across your website, Mr. Riley."

He corrected me, "Everyone calls me 'G.' Including my parents. In Jamaica, they like to give the kids pet names, and mine has been 'G' for as long as I can remember."

"It seems that time demands are subject to the foundation practices that you identified in your article about email. Arriving, Deciding, Deleting, Completing Now, Keeping and Listing." He nodded and broke out in a wide smile.

"Time demands come into our lives, and we act on them using certain forces. What's missing from the whole discussion is the fact that we do that in different ways - each of us has individual methods and unique ways of working through time demands, even as we use the foundation practices."

Andre asked, "Is there something wrong with that?" He sounded just a little defensive.

"No," I explained, "RingCORE has it right in this regard. It's not enough, however. When people are left to their own devices, they end up running off the rails. Instead, they need some help. What they can be given is a variation of what G has invented. Not just six foundation practices, but a ladder of skills within each of the 6 so that they can evaluate themselves... figure out which ones are weak and which ones need to be improved."

When I paused to make sure that I was making sense to them, G added, "It seems to me that with the right tool, each person could evaluate and understand their current system by coming up with something like a report card, or a profile. A good tool would show them not only where they are, but also where they need to improve to become masterful."

Andre nodded and said, "That would be awesome to have. It would put them in charge of their own evaluation and development, as they work on their areas of greatest improvement. The profiles would likely differ greatly from one person to the next."

I agreed. "Yes, and that's because we are each left on our own when we are teens or young adults to come up with ways to deal with time demands. Without a map of the entire picture, each of us puts together piecemeal solutions by trial and error. And then, if we stop experimenting, we end up stuck in one single pattern. What we really need to do is to keep evolving all the time."

G noted, "And that's why gadget sales are soaring, but crazy habits are increasing even faster. On the way here, I saw a lady texting while driving - weaving all around the road. I drove by and gave her my best angry look, but she didn't even notice." He showed us "the look" and we both laughed.

"Right," I said. "When you haven't learned about the foundations and time demands, you don't know how to put an effective upgrade in place. Buying a new device should be the last thing that you do. Imagine RingCORE running to the latest trade show to purchase the newest gaming technology before deciding whether or not we need it. Most smartphone purchases are made that way. Same for tablets, laptops - any new shiny stuff."

A thoughtful silence fell over our little meeting.

Andre broke it with an explanation for G. "Bill here is on loan from Syscon -- I'm on good terms with their CEO. He's an expert in a new learning technology called Zebon, but it looks as if he has some other tricks up his sleeve."

G asked, "How much longer will you be around RingCORE, Bill?"

"Well, the loan is only for twelve months, so I have about seven left. I hope to connect these ideas in a way that affects the way we implement Zebon."

Andre cut in, "That's going to change. Bill, one of the reasons I wanted to talk with you is that I got a surprise from Syscon last night. They've asked for you to come back early. I tried to keep you here with us to put the Zebon ideas into production, but that's not to be. You'll be back in about a month, it seems."

It was the last thing I wanted to hear.

* * *

*Can't anything go right?*

The weight of my shoulders bore down, and I could feel them sag. I'm sure my face did also, as my two colleagues stared.

Dry mouth. Pulsing temples. Breath stuck in my throat. *Oh God, No.*

Andre carefully offered, "It looks like you have some mixed feelings about going back?"

I nodded.

"Between you and me, the news coming out of there isn't good. Let's just say that they are desperately trying to prevent another layoff, but productivity is so low that..."

G asked, "Have you been affected by any of this?"

"Affected?" I repeated ruefully, trying to play off my disappointment before it started to seep out. Well, the seepage turned into a pour and then a torrent as I shared everything. A few times, stopping myself looked like a really good idea, but the way they listened so intently... I wasn't done until I had told the story of the layoff list, the mysterious email, the continuous threats, doing the jobs of Anna and Joe. Martha, Vernon, Manuel plus my attempts with the BrainPhone. Sandy too.

*Stop.* I should have quit after a quick summary.

Andre, "It's been tough. It sounds like you were happy to come here to escape."

They were the first people in the world to grasp everything, yet I hardly knew them.

"It sounds awful," G summarized. Andre nodded in agreement. They both sat there looking at me before he continued, "But it's clear that you must go back."

Andre intoned, "It ....is... your.... destiny." They both looked at each other and at me. And burst out laughing. These two were apparently closer than brothers, because they began playing with Obi Wan and Darth Vader voices, seeing who could outdo the other in a geeky aside that surprised the heck out of me.

As a Star Wars fan, I couldn't help but laugh, too; I was shocked to see these two men, whom I'd come to respect so much, acting just like kids. "But seriously Bill, it's the right thing for you to do. While we're a fine company to run away to, your life needs to be worked out back at Syscon. It's not a bad place, I don't think, but it's been through hard times; everyone will benefit if you can make a big difference."

He paused, as if he wasn't sure how I'd react.

It was blowing my mind. *Making a big difference*? I thought. That damn phrase was now flapping in my face. "At Syscon?" I asked out aloud.

But as the words left my lips, I caught a glimpse of how small and petty I had become. All I'd had before coming to RingCORE were fears. Just a few minutes ago, we were talking about ideas that could change the way RingCORE employees managed their time, balanced their lives, and dealt with the stress that many who left were still bitter about.

As if reading my mind, G added, "The bigger question is, who or what are you for?" His deep voice emphasized the word "for."

"Well, I'm against losing my job, the house. I don't want another round of Sandy's depression to ever hurt her again. Looking bad in front of other people. I also don't want to fail at being a provider."

"But who or what are you for, not just against?" Andre also emphasized the word "for."

"I...I... have forgotten all about that way of thinking. I know what I don't want. But what am I for?" I took a deep breath and sighed before continuing.

"Well, being here at RingCORE has been great because I have found something to care about. It's been bigger than I have found in years – making sense of people's productivity and time management. Syscon forced me to try to get better, but until I knew I was coming here, all I discovered were ways that didn't work. Now, answers and solutions are actually coming. I could turn that into some kind of destiny, right?"

They nodded and smiled like a couple of Cheshire cats. Then came more Star Wars re-enactments with lines from Yoda and his younglings. I liked the movies, but I couldn't recite them.

For a moment, I felt like more than just a desperate, insignificant little engineer in New Jersey. I felt different.

# Chapter 11

Standing in the doorway of Andre's office, I stopped for a moment. Looking around the secretarial pool, I nodded confidently to the administrative assistants at their work stations, thinking that the executive suite was a heady place for a meeting. With a long, purposeful stride, I made my way to the end of the corridor. Andre, G and I agreed that I had made an important start, so we set up a series of Sunday evening calls to keep the momentum. RingCORE needed to realize a tangible benefit from what we had begun, and there was a lot more work to do.

When I turned the corner, it all evaporated. *Syscon. The consultants' report. Nick Holleran. Vernon. Too many Project Managers.* All of my old fears rushed back in.

The hallways were dimly lit as I plodded over the well-worn industrial carpet. It needed to be replaced. Something should be done to brighten up the place. The nerdy people I passed were no masters of social skills - lots of them only stared when I wished them good morning or good afternoon. And their clothes... nothing that a match and some lighter-fluid wouldn't fix. Why didn't they fix up the place? Before the meeting, I hadn't realized how much of an upgrade it needed. Now...

*I need to clear my head.*

There was a department meeting scheduled to start in just a few minutes, but when I got to the end of my division's corridor, I strode right past. Why not take the tour of the building I had promised myself on my very first day? That might bring me back to the inspiration I'd left behind in Andre's office.

As I stretched my legs and walked quickly from one corridor to the next, I poked my head into a lab here and an office there to see some of the intriguing things that were being invented. RingCORE employees loved to place displays, graphs, pictures and models in plain sight where others could see them. It was their way of sharing their work with the wider world, and it made the place into a mini-museum. Just the kind of distraction I needed.

When I got to the first floor of Building One, the sign for the Human Resources department loomed overhead. I almost skipped it - HR Departments aren't usually cutting-edge. Certainly, there would be no lab.

*Wrong.* At the end of the corridor, there was a poster demonstration sponsored by RingCORE HR Labs. A handful of employees were milling around, moving from one poster to another. I joined in as my curiosity piqued.

The first poster was all about the guy who wrote *Flow: The Psychology of Optimal Experience* - Mihaly Csikszentmihalyi. The book was sitting on my Kindle, unfinished, but my brief research had filled me in on its broader themes. The next poster showed research from the other book that Mike mentioned - *Peopleware*, by DeMarco and Lister. The authors were foundational thinkers for the company's vision of a hyper-productive workplace that gave employees an opportunity to do their best work. According to the authors, it was a way for people to be happy and fulfilled, but not in a general sense. Flow talked about an ecstatic, peak experience that occurs doing your best work.

Beyond these two were posters with statements of the company's long term improvement plans, built on the standices that already were in place.

RingCORE was in the middle of executing a fifteen-year blueprint to transform its physical surroundings using these authors' findings. It took them a long time to move from being a cubicle farm just like Syscon to a system of private or two-person offices. Now, they could slip into the most productive states, described by Csikszentmihalyi and DeMarco and Lister, whenever they wanted.

Smartphone abuse posters took up several panels and described some recent efforts to research the impact of electronic distractions on employee productivity. All of their findings made perfect sense. I thought it should be mandatory for all new users to read that stuff - smartphones, like cigarettes, should be labeled. "Warning - the use of this device while driving a car at any speed can kill children in school buses!"

The last set of panels showed RingCORE's evolution over the years, using photos and even a few video clips on LCD screens. It was cool to see them transform the workplace in small steps, doing experiments here and there to discover what would lower costs and raise productivity. A ten-year-old picture of G and Andre working together on a task force caught me by surprise. They had been partners in building a great company for longer than I realized. Seeing younger versions of the two of them made me see that the quiet, busy hum that I loved about the place hadn't come about by accident.

In fact, that was the point of the posters. The productive environment I'd stumbled upon was not a lucky coincidence, but it been designed consciously, and it had taken some smart people several years of steady effort to craft. The company had studied many new ideas, slowly turning them into established practices that guys like me took for granted. It made that "big difference" they talked about.

Returning to my office, I chose to take the long route, chewing over the meeting and the content of the posters in my mind. RingCORE reminded me of the companies I read about in books like "Built to Last" by Jim Collins; they described companies that took a long, vision-driven view. These companies were far more successful than their mediocre counterparts, which failed to think far ahead or see the big picture.

Just like mediocre me. *Far ahead? Big picture?*

I was failing in exactly the same way. What had I accomplished in the last two or three years?

What was my big picture?

One of the posters, featuring Albert Einstein, popped into my head. Taking a shortcut back to the HR Labs poster demo I swung around the panels until I found what I was looking for.

Under a classic black and white photo of the famed genius was printed, "Only a life lived for others is a life worthwhile." Behind that panel, another featured the reggae singer Bob Marley and the words, "The greatness of a man is not in how much wealth he acquires, but in his integrity and his ability to affect those around him positively."

I stared at Marley's face. He died in the early eighties before becoming a global icon. Einstein made history as a physicist but became known for much more than just an equation. And here I was, clinging to my job in New Jersey, living on fumes for longer than I could remember.

The look on the faces of Andre and G, pushing me to save more than just my own skin... I suddenly felt ashamed. I shook my head, trying to erase the memory, and a young lady walking by gave me a strange look, but I didn't care. Her opinion of me was a small thing. But I did dart down a corridor just in case she came back for a second look.

If her opinion of me was a small thing, how about the others? RingCORE opinions. Syscon opinions. Andre, Mike or G. Or Martha, Vernon or Ted. Or Sandy or the kids. I couldn't even be trusted with a reliable opinion of myself, I smirked wryly.

Then, what was the point of attending to all these small things? G and Andre showed me how liberating it was to focus on big things... ideas that could change an entire company and maybe even more. I could join them in the effort to make a difference. A big difference.

The sun was shining on the east side of the building, and it started to get warmer as I picked up the pace. The words were coming faster now... *a big difference.* The corridors were lit better now, so I could see through the windows that the parking lot was brightly lit up with the morning sun.

*How could I hold on to this feeling?*

I ignored this and other questions for a minute and went back a step. *What matters—what big stuff should I be sweating instead of the small stuff?* That wasn't too hard to figure out. I loved making people more productive, testing out new ideas, and watching them make a difference. My time at RingCORE had made that clear - this was the purest opportunity I ever had to put time and energy into that commitment. Ever since my shift, I remained on the lookout for tools that would help my team mates in the DAPE project get better at their time management while escaping Vernon's my-way-or-the-highway approach.

There must be others at Syscon and other places who were doing the jobs of several people. Their families were paying the price: they bought smartphones like I did, hoping they would help, and they tried partial solutions like MTM to tell them what to do. The Employee Productivity Study showed that we were way behind. This was all wrong, wrong, wrong. What was I going to do about this?

What would it be like to transport some of the focused, joyful experiences of doing great work from RingCORE over to Syscon? What if that freedom to function at a high level was available? What would happen to all that fear?

Frankly, I was afraid of the answer.

I took a deep breath. Was it worth losing my job over? That pang of fear ran through me just as I spoke out aloud, "My job has been to keep my job." An older Asian fellow snapped his head to look at me carefully, because I wasn't quiet.

Not caring but laughing out loud, I said, "I'm fired!" Trump would have been proud. "I'm going to kick myself out of the job of trying to keep my job. If I lose my job at Syscon, then so be it." I rarely swear, but this time I almost did.

*I quit.*

* * *

The downtown hotel in Phoenix was nice -- better than anything Syscon had ever allowed me to stay in. It was situated in a cluster of modern buildings; when my taxi pulled up, my eyes brightened just a bit as I conjured up a picture of the interior based on its eye-catching, glass shielded facade. The mid-May sun was setting early in the sky as I jumped out of the cab and made my way to the lobby.

When I got to my room, I wasn't disappointed. RingCORE was obviously, doing well so it could afford to place its employees in business hotels that gave a little lift, rather than dulled the spirits with cheap interiors, funky smells and long commutes into downtown (the Syscon way).

Arriving early for an Ohara project team review on Monday morning, I wanted to make the most of my third call with G and Andre. Their constant joking around made our conversations turn into a light-hearted give and take, with me doing most of the taking. They called me "The Serious One" in tones that echoed another favorite movie - The Matrix.

Every time they repeated my new nickname, I felt chills - but not because I disliked the name. Instead, it reminded me of my vow to quit the job of trying to keep my job, helping me to remember what I was really about. In those moments, I could relax and believe that any outcome to my career aspirations would be just the perfect one. All of this made the calls effortless.

After settling in, I sat at the amply supplied business desk and logged onto Skype, waiting for the others to show up.

"Hey, guys," I said as they made their way onto the call at almost the same time. They each had their video cameras turned on, so I did the same. As usual, they were in a good mood.

"What's happening, gentlemen? Shall we get into it? We agreed to look at the reasons why people at RingCORE struggle to become more productive."

"I have a few insights," I explained. "While the company allows employees to choose how they approach time management, it doesn't actually help them do anything except stay in the same place. In other words, there's no easy way to improve their skills, even if they want to. All they have in front of them is a vague target, even though they might have knowledge of the foundation practices."

The other guys fell silent, as we usually did when listening to something unusual or different. Our conversations were the only ones I ever had where silence seemed to be as important as talking.

"What more do they need? I don't understand that." That was G's voice.

I decided to try for a comparison. "I don't know much about golf, but the little I see from television tells me that there are a bunch of intricate skills involved, so if I were to pick up the game I'd need a way to develop them simultaneously from the ground up."

"Well," said Andre, "I have been playing for a few years and I have developed a pretty good drive, but my putting stinks. Guess which one I have to focus on?"

G added, "That seems to be a more realistic example. You don't have people who enter RingCore with absolutely no time management skills whatsoever. They never would have graduated from college. Instead, they come with a mix of skills... some sharp, but some under-developed. If they came as blank slates, it would be easier, as you could put everyone through a beginner-level class and be done with it. In academic circles it's known as "andragogy" - the teaching of adult learners who come with some knowledge or skills. Pedagogy, on the other hand, involves teaching kids who are brand new to a subject."

"Last year, I went to a golf camp near Las Vegas," Andre added. "The first thing they did at the start of the two weeks was do an assessment. None of us were beginners, and the problems I saw were all over the map. Each of us needed an individual program, based on where we were starting." He paused. "And also where we were going. There were a few teenagers who were desperately trying to become the next Tiger Woods, and they might not have been better than the rest of us, but they certainly improved more quickly. One kid lost five strokes during the week."

I asked, "Did they give you a report in Vegas? When they did the initial assessment?"

"Yeah, let me send it to you guys." After a few minutes, we were looking at his score-sheet, which listed a bunch of skills and his ranking in each one. He was very good at things like "the long game," "distance and "accuracy" but awful at "putting" and "the short game," just as he had said. Beside each skill there was a list of proficiency levels ranging from 1 to 10.

However, some other intriguing indicators caught my attention. "Are these your targets for each skill?" I stared at another chart that set up a plan for developing each skill. It had target dates for him to move from his current level of proficiency to the next and then to the next.

"That's right. They expected us to make some quantum leaps during camp, but afterwards we would expect to see slower gains. That's my 24 month plan you're looking at."

"24 months? How have you been doing?" I asked. "Did you hit your targets?"

He took a moment to answer. "For about six months, I did really well. Another guy who also went to the camp lived about a block from my home, and we kept each other straight. That is, until he moved to Kentucky. After that, I haven't had the discipline. Obviously, it's all his fault." That quip got a guffaw, and he added, "If I want to get any better, I'll have to pay him to come back."

When our laughter stopped, it led to more silence. I could almost hear our collective wheels turning.

"If we were to look at all the participants in your golf camp, they'd each have different score-sheets and target dates, but they'd all be moving in the same direction," I said.

"At very different speeds," Andre added.

G asked, "Is there a description of the difference between proficiency levels 4 and 5 in putting?"

"Yeah," Andre answered. "It's all laid out in excruciating detail on their website, just so that guys like me don't fool ourselves into thinking we're better than we really are."

G and I answered excitedly at the same time, but I was a bit louder. "What the heck is stopping us from doing the same thing here? We can follow the same format, but instead apply it to the foundations in order to create our own proficiency levels with just as much detail as we want."

G responded, "It might work. It would be a big improvement over the standard approach of simply handing someone a fixed set of practices and wishing them good luck. That's what MTM and every other book does."

Andre asked, "But does that mean we have to go around diagnosing every single person individually? That's what we did in Las Vegas, and it required a whole team of pros. That wasn't cheap." Out loud, he started multiplying the number of coaches RingCORE would need by their salaries plus overheads, then announced, "That equals... more than we can afford."

"We don't have that luxury. What we must do is find a way to teach each person how to do their own diagnosis," I suggested. "Maybe that can be done in the right training program. After that, they just need to work with someone who won't leave for Kentucky."

We all laughed. It broke the tense effort we had been putting in for the past hour, and we relaxed as Andre told us a joke about a local politician. I laughed, but couldn't prevent a creeping sadness. This was my last call before returning to Syscon.

Andre returned us to the topic at hand, "I don't know how we can even do that. That sounds like it would be a hard trick to pull off. And it could take years to get the average RingCORE employee to be able to assess their own skills with that kind of precision?"

"It would be difficult," G answered. "We'd have to do a lot of work to equip them with the right technique and tools. I don't know if it can be done this way. It's much easier to get a lot of skilled coaches involved, then follow the golf camp model."

Andre continued, "Well, it's easier but not affordable. We need to find a way to show them how to assess themselves to build their own change plan. What more would they need?

I added, "They'd need their own guy in Kentucky. A way to ensure that they stayed on track for the long haul. Most people are weak when it comes to implementing long-term behavior changes, even when they claim to be motivated. Remember the heart attack victims."

"That's what the training would also have to address," said G. "If they are weak in making change permanent, then we need to make them strong. There's a bunch of research out there on mastering these complex skills, starting with a book I just read - *Outliers*, by Malcolm Gladwell."

"I'm not aware of any time management or productivity training that goes this far -- instead, they dump a long list of changes in your lap and, in effect, announce that you're "good to go." Lots of training programs do that, actually," G complained.

After a short pause, Andre brought us back to reality - "So, what's our next step, guys? Are you still planning to leave RingCORE, Bill?" He sounded just a little disappointed this time.

*Planning to leave? What choice did I have?* "Yes, in a couple of weeks I'll be back at Syscon."

"Listen, Bill, I'm seeing your CEO tomorrow night for dinner. I'm sure I could twist his arm into extending your stay for another 3 months, or maybe even a whole lot more -- he owes me some big favors. What do you think?"

I gasped quietly. *Here it is. My chance to stay at RingCORE.*

"In fact, he continued, I have an open position coming up here at RingCORE that I'd like you to apply for."

Before I could consider his offer, I heard a voice say, "I'd love to, but I need to get back to Syscon in order to help spread some of what I've learned here at RingCORE. Management thinks it needs to cut staff to boost productivity and save the company. It does need improvement, and it's more urgent than ever before given the recent financials. But there's another way. We can grow our people's time management skills and become more individually productive, teaching them how to live more balanced lives at the same time. It doesn't have to be as bad as it is right now... things could be much better, and improved time management is one of the keys to accomplishing anything worthwhile. Everything."

*Who the hell just said all that?*

This time, the silence was filled with something else I didn't feel very often. A sense of responsibility and a hint of appreciation.

"I wish I could convince you to stay. We are onto something that could make a big difference here at RingCORE - a natural extension of the ideas we have been working on for a long time. Over a decade. But it's good that you care so much and that you're willing to take a stand."

G asked, "Will you still be able to make our calls? We have a long way to go in order to convert our ideas into real results. I need some standices to put into play to move my folks to the next level."

"Of course. What would you guys do without the Serious One?" I said, and it drew a laugh from them both.

We said our goodbyes, and I turned to the mirror to see myself standing just a bit taller, with a steady gaze at something that I hardly recognized: a sense of purpose.

* * *

My last few days at RingCore were a sprint, as I tried to share as much as I could about Zebon before leaving. It didn't hurt that my Tzinbox score registered a +9 for the first time, telling me that I was on top of things in spite of the rush I was in.

A young woman in Phoenix took over my role on the Ohara project. I could tell from her energy that it would be in good hands, as she was on her way to knowing just as much as I did about Zebon.

Before leaving, I filled up every spare hour in an attempt to bring the conversation that G, Andre and I had on Sunday night to closure. Early one Wednesday morning, I set some time aside to get into the flow state.

Starting with G's foundation actions, I set them aside for a new model based on what I called "the fundamental practices of time management." Like Einstein, my new hero, I'd do my best to discover a theory that united the way humans handled time demands from all sources.

Using Andre's golf training materials and some competency development models from the Internet, I went back to my little episode at the karate school. The belt system in the martial arts provided the perfect example of a ladder of skills, so, even though I looked around for better models, I decided to use it. Other disciplines like Six Sigma were already using a belt system, and I hesitated. I chose it because everyone understood that the difference between white belts and black belts was a big one that involved a lot of steps.

To start to define a list of robust practices I went back to watching old auto assembly videos on YouTube. Then, I began to imagine what happened to a time demand once it entered someone's life. How did people with different skills deal with it? How did it get acted on? Or lost?

The first fundamental I came up with was Capturing, which was the same term that G used. I ended up with a similar list to his foundations: seven practices that included Capturing, Emptying, Tossing, Acting Now, Storing, Scheduling, and Listing. None of them required any particular technology, as they comprised habits, practices and rituals of different kinds.

After surveying a few time management and productivity books as well as a number of websites, I decided that these seven practices were the only ones that we applied to time demands, in order to move them along in our lives. I started writing furiously - after all, I only had a few days left, and I believed that once I returned to Syscon, the pixie dust I had picked up at RingCORE would simply vanish.

My end product had lots of gaps. Pinning down details, like the differences between yellow and orange belts in "Storing," was tough. I had to use my imagination to fill some of the holes. It had been a random stumble over the years and putting the ladders down on paper showed me where I still had lots of room to improve.

Black belts, I decided, were out of everyone's reach at this point. I labeled the black belt as "to be defined." By putting a black belt out of reach, no one could claim that the 7 Ladders were the "final" answer to time management and personal productivity. After my work, I came up with only four belts: White, Yellow, Orange and Green.

When I finally stopped, it was 6 p.m. I had worked through the entire day, eating a brown bag lunch somewhere along the way. My neck and back were both stiff.

Finally, I sent an email to G and Andre entitled "The 7 Ladders." Mike was copied; so was Martha for good measure.

The following morning, I started packing my office into brown cardboard boxes, a sure sign to anyone that I'd be leaving soon.

As I started putting away my stuff, I heard a knock on the door, which was ajar. That was just the beginning of what turned into a day of long goodbyes and very little packing. Apparently, Mike had sent around the highlights of what I had written along with a note saying that I'd be leaving. I heard the phrase "7 Ladders" about ten or fifteen times that day from people who thanked me for what I'd written – it had gone viral. Some were surprised, as if they didn't know that I had it in me to put together something so "different."

Those were the buzzwords of the day; "different" and "7 Ladders."

Even Andre came by and, once again, hinted that I didn't need to leave so quickly, or permanently. Once again, that voice came out of nowhere to declare, "It's simply the right thing to do."

It no longer shocked me, but it wasn't entirely comfortable to hear, even if it wasn't coming out of nowhere anymore. Some of my fears had slipped aside to allow something else to emerge, and yes... it really was my voice.

With the memo complete, I felt that my last obligation to RingCORE was complete. In a conversation with Ted, I admitted, "I'm actually looking forward to returning to Syscon. Even though it's a tough environment, I have something useful to offer. Staying here at RingCORE would be nice, but it's not where my commitment lies. Not really."

He snorted in response and said "Good luck with it, Moses. Just don't die in the wilderness, okay?"

The next day, I got into the office early to find an email from Martha. She asked me to put together a short message for the company newsletter on my experience at RingCORE - more to satisfy everyone's curiosity than to share hardcore content. With the door closed, I spent a couple of hours on the article before finishing the last of my packing.

After carrying my stuff to the car, I drove away from RingCORE for the last time as an employee-on-loan. A last-day-of-class, last-day-of-vacation feeling came over me as I left behind a bunch of new friends and a company that was heads and shoulders above any others I had seen first-hand.

Nodding and half-waving at the building as I circled the parking lot, I imagined parking my car in the Syscon lot before entering the building the following week. It would be the right thing to do, I told myself for the umpteenth time, even if it came at a possible cost.

I felt bigger and stronger than I had in years.

* * *

============================
**Bill Crossley**
-----------------------------------------------
From: Bill.Crossley@syscon.com
To: Andre.Anderson@RingCORE.com, Graham.Riley@Cornell.edu
CC: Martha.Adelman@syscon.com, Mike.Springer@RingCORE.com
Subject: The 7 Ladders and Time Demands

I have proposed the following seven practices (please note that this is a bit of a departure from G's original work.)
1. Capturing
2. Emptying
3. Tossing
4. Acting Now
5. Storing
6. Scheduling
7. Listing

From where I stand, people have developed different levels of skill in each of these core practices. To help in their assessment, I imagine seven distinct ladders, each ranging from novice to expert. Each ladder corresponds to one of these practices. It's easy for someone to be an expert in one practice and a novice in another.

Here is a synopsis of how they work together.

As I mentioned to you before, time demands come into our lives from a number of places, triggered by the events in our lives. As they get created and arrive in our lives, they are temporarily stored as Capture Points in a process called "Capturing."

Think of a factory that makes cars. The individual autos are time demands, which are created 24-7. Then, imagine Capture Points as a huge system of parking lots in which finished cars are parked temporarily.

Once they are parked, they sit waiting for someone to take an action. In the same way, some of our personal Capture Points are automatic and collect time demands all day and night. Examples include email Inboxes, Twitter accounts, PO Boxes, text messages, instant messages, etc. Others are manual and involve our active involvement, such as our personal memory, a paper pad, a smartphone, a digital voice-recorder, and such like.

The best time managers rarely use memory as a Capture Point and instead use other techniques that tend to be more reliable.

Back to the parking lot / Capture Point. At different moments in time, someone shows up and starts moving cars to different destinations. They not only empty the lot, but they also make a decision about each car's next destination.

In much the same way, time demands are removed from our Capture Points in a deliberate, conscious process of Emptying. This is also a moment of decision, when we mentally do something with the time demands. Skillful professionals do this step well and leave their Capture Points empty. Novices end up with overflowing Capture Points and a great deal of mental stress, especially if they habitually use their memory as a Capture Point.

When we Empty a Capture Point, we must take one of five actions: Tossing, Acting Now, Storing, Scheduling and Listing.

When we Toss, we void the time demand entirely, destroying it.

When we Act Now, we take immediate action, but limit the amount of time we spend on an action to less than five minutes.

When we Store, we save important information for later possible use, although we may not know when it will be used - like a phone number.

When we Schedule, we place a time demand directly into our calendar.

When we List, we place a time demand directly onto a task or to-do list.

Once we get around to executing a time demand successfully, it vanishes. Sometimes, its completion may lead to the creation of new ones. For example, sending an email report to the team might lead me to set up a meeting to discuss its contents.

Guys, I have struggled to think of other ways that we manage time demands, but can't think of any. From my knowledge of MTM and other books and programs, I can see that these 7 Fundamentals are at the core of every time management system, like a skeleton embedded in the core of every human body. They cannot be escaped, even by people who don't know that they are using a commercial system of habits, practices and rituals described by a guru.

Some final observations about these 7 Ladders...

**Observation #1** - most of us develop our own time management skills without the help of a class or book and end up with an uneven set of ladders – we're experts in some fundamental practices and novices in others.

**Observation #2** - by the time we get around to taking a class as adults, it's too late. We have already practiced our self-developed, unique method for many years and find it hard to change.

**Observation #3** - most classes and books are all about sharing one, single pattern of practices that their creators discovered and found to be useful. They do a good job of describing their approach, and they attempt to get everyone else to follow their method of executing each of the 7 Fundamentals. Sometimes this approach works for some people, but it fails for most.

**Observation #4** - these creators unintentionally leave their trainees stuck, because they don't offer an upgrade or a next step. In their class or book, they present their particular pattern of practice as the be-all-end-all solution. If you want to make further improvements, you are on your own. But life just doesn't remain the same... along comes a technology, change, or a new set of time demands (e.g. having a baby), and with it comes a fresh pair of eyes and a need to upgrade and adjust.

**Observation #5** - people fail when they try to become experts in all the fundamentals too quickly. They are better off taking baby steps.

Here is an example of what a "Capturing Ladder" might look like, with different skill levels. Remember, this only applies to time demands like "remember the milk," not other stuff we need to remember, like the capital of Wisconsin.

Capturing Skill - White Belt - uses memory all the time as a Capture Point for time demands, making them unreliable because things get forgotten. They also poorly manage email, Twitter DM's, Facebook messages, letters, memos, bills and text messages.

Capturing Skill - Yellow Belt - uses memory some of the time, but supplements it with the occasional piece of paper: better at managing electronic messages and paper than someone at Rung 1.

Capturing Skill - Green Belt - never uses memory. They always write down time demands or put them in their smartphone. They perfectly manage the flow of time demands coming at them in electronic messages of all kinds and also on paper.

I'm nowhere near a Green Belt, but I have met a few people who are close. Maybe Mike is one? I got stuck trying to define a Capturing Skill Orange Belt and left it out because I ran out of time and energy. Imagine something like this for all seven practices - a self-diagnostic that would pick up the flaws that we unintentionally introduced when we developed our own time management system.

This 7-Ladder summary makes me realize how complex time management behaviors really are, and it explains why lists of sexy tips and tricks don't work. It's also why flashy new technology often fails to do more than entertain us – new devices hardly ever help us to move up a single rung.

I'm beat. This is as far as I could get, but I'll bet there's a lot more that I didn't cover. Let me know what you think.

Bill

------------------------------------------

# Chapter 12

Martha's office was almost the same as I remembered. She had some new pictures of her kids and a couple of new inspirational posters. New stacks of paper interrupted the carpet, and the piles on her desk seemed higher than before.

It was good to be back on familiar turf; I did have some great memories here. It was impossible to forget the tough conversations, however. Lists and layoffs. I couldn't forget them, but they were a bit further away than ever before. Maybe it was because I had been away? Or perhaps it had something to do with my decision to never allow my life to become over-focused on a single, fear-filled goal. Once in this lifetime was enough.

*It won't happen again.*

Maybe if I said that over and over again, it wouldn't. Now, all I needed was a pair of red shoes, a little black dog and a home in Kansas to complete the trick.

My mind drifted back to a conversation I'd had with Sandy last night.

"Are you sure that going back is a good idea?" she asked with a knowing look. "You have been so happy at RingCORE."

"Actually, it has been pretty good. But I needed to return to Syscon eventually. The timing is right because I learned a lot at RingCORE to take back and have even come up with some new things to make people work better."

"What was it like before?" she asked. Once again, she looked me right in the eye, lingering a bit, as if already she knew everything.

"Just stressful stuff that people have a hard time dealing with." Now, I sounded vague and stupid to my own ears. But I stuck to my guns. *Got to follow Roma's rules.*

She looked surprisingly pained and started to say something, but stopped. She took a deep breath, "Yesterday, I read in the papers that things are tougher than ever for engineers and scientists in the Tri-State area. Honey, you know that you can tell me anything, right?"

I don't know what look came across my face, but I could feel my eyes welling up. Fighting back a tear, I swallowed. Every instinct I possessed told me to sit down and share everything. She'd be understanding and caring. We'd put together a plan to deal with whatever fallout might take place if things took a turn for the worse. We'd do it together, the way a husband and wife should.

But I bit my lip. *Damned Dr. Roma.* The advice given in his Miami office was blunt and simple. There was no mistaking it if I wanted to prevent those dark curtains. Someone had to take care of Lizzy and Rebecca. My mother hadn't been able to take care of herself when she was depressed, let alone us kids.

*No way.*

Her eyes opened wide and she looked at me expectantly. *Not now. When it's all over.*

I took a moment and said "Of course I know that; we're a team of two." That phrase was one that we used to say all the time when we were dating and hadn't used in years. She hugged me and said, "Yeah, we are. You just remember that, okay?"

"Ah, Bill, welcome back." The voice that interrupted my reverie in Martha's office wasn't hers, and I spun around in the chair to find Vernon looking over me. He looked different than I remembered. Shorter and older. He even appeared to have put on weight. He still had the habit of standing just a little too close.

"Thanks, Vernon -- to be honest I have mixed feelings about being back here."

"Oh, why is that?" he said with a smirk. Our last conversation flashed into my mind. It looked as if he remembered it also, as his eyes simmered.

Before I could answer, Martha came in the door with a breezy "Hi, Bill -- it's good to have you back! I thought we had lost you there for a while!" I laughed, but Vernon's face remained in a stiff half-smile.

We made some small talk about my experience at RingCORE, but I didn't let on much. Where would I start? It would all come out in time.

"By the way, good job in improving that Tzinbox score. You went from a -9 to a +9 in no time! Even a 10 now and then.... Being away from here did you well, huh?" Martha smiled as she patted me on the back.

This took me a bit by surprise, and then I recalled that those statistics were reported to managers. She had never mentioned it in conversation before, and I had never thought she noticed.

"Well, thanks. It wasn't hard, given their culture." They both looked interested, but Martha glanced at the clock before abruptly announcing, "Let me cut to the chase. Bill, Vernon's DAPE project has evolved to the point where we need to make some decisions. The project has now become the company's number one priority; there's a sub-system called Alpha that he needs to focus on with a special team. Basically he needs to split the project."

She went on to explain the technical reasons it needed to happen this way, and I glanced at Vernon. Now, he was really smiling, looking pleased.

"What I propose is that you both report to me, with Vernon focusing on Alpha, and Bill... you'll head up the Beta Team, which has everything else. On your team, you'll have... hold on a minute, let me pull it up." She went into her email to grab a list of names.

As she read them off, my heart sank. She could not have picked a weaker team. If there was ever a group formed of those "Most Likely to be Voted Out of Syscon," then this would be it. Didn't she notice that Vernon had taken all the obvious talent for the Alpha team?

I took a deep breath and let it out slowly. Some cool new air brought me back to my bigger goals.

"How about Ted?" I asked, "Where is he in all this? He'd be great to have on this team because of his background."

"Vernon, where is Ted?" she echoed.

He looked suspiciously at the two of us. "He's on my team, but he's been very unproductive lately. He doesn't even try to follow MTM and keeps on doing his own thing. If you think he could help your team, then by all means..."

"To be successful, I'll need Ted, plus a few things." Martha and Vernon looked at me carefully. "We're going to need quiet space to focus. We can't do this kind of work in open cubicles."

"That's not how we work around here," Vernon burst out. His irritated tone caught Martha's attention, and she turned her head slowly to look at him. She focused on him deliberately with a face of complete calm. Silence hung heavily in the air as he awkwardly tried to fill the gap she had just provoked.

"Martha, that article that Bill wrote was utter nonsense. It's against everything we do around here -- there's simply no place at Syscon for these techniques that Bill dug up. My team isn't going to go through a bunch of new experimentation for no reason. We have been doing fine up until now with our own methods and don't need to learn anything new from the outside that doesn't mesh with our culture. There's a right way and a wrong way to do things; he's obviously following some of the wrong ways or he wouldn't be back here so soon."

Martha allowed his rant to hang in the air.

"Xavier Kripanali clearly states that productivity has nothing to do with one's physical environment or the tools you use and that it's all about frame of mind. This article is completely against MTM and everything that makes sense -- if he believes these things, then I don't think he's fit to lead a team." He spat out these last words with an angry fervor that made us stare at him.

*He's lost a screw.*

Once again, Martha didn't respond to him. She paused, took a breath, and calmly looked away from Vernon as if he were speaking a foreign language. "Actually, guys, I read both documents carefully. Bill, what else do you need?" she asked.

As I answered with as many details as I could, she made a list and promised to follow up with an email outlining the costs.

Five minutes later, we left her office, and Vernon was wearing a glassy, cold mask.

* * *

The Beta team was in a mid-morning brainstorming session, but I was quiet, trying to figure out a way to move the team forward. The ideas being thrown back and forth weren't very good at all.

I sat back in my chair, just watching the give and take. On one side of the table sat Kumar, Debi and David while on the other, Frankie, Betty and Brandy were standing at the white board, trying to get a point across using colored markers and a great deal of gusto. Ted sat at the other end of the table, and his eyes caught mine with a distinct twinkle. He loved these sessions, he kept saying, partly because they were so dramatic and partly because they were short.

Beta was now using the RingCORE practice of keeping short meetings that turned into intense exchanges of ideas and points of view, some of the highest-quality conversations I had ever witnessed at Syscon.

My meeting with Martha and Vernon was a month in the past, and the team was located in our new headquarters. Everything on my list was provided, including a novel office setup that gave everyone in the team some quiet privacy and access to a shared space for meetings at any time. It would have been quite normal at RingCORE, but at Syscon it created quite a buzz. We got all sorts of unwanted attention, as people commented about our setup and the "perks" that we had been granted.

While that was an important aspect of our approach, it was a small thing compared to how far we had to go to reach the RingCORE standard. Meetings could never start on time. If they did, someone was missing. Email was used as a backup tool for verbal requests, because so many time demands just weren't tracked after they were created. Promises that were made fell off people's radars only to be resurrected in moments of crisis.

It came as no surprise when we discovered, in the second week, that we had all fallen on the wrong side of Vernon. More than half of the team openly cringed when I brought up the idea of working on the team's capacity for results using improvements in time management. When I asked "What's going on?" out came tales of being sidelined while attending MTM workshops before being labeled as troublemakers and contrarians. The word got back to Vernon, who only increased the pressure on them to conform. There had been a lot of one-way coaching sessions in my absence.

When I shared the 7 Ladders Memo with the team, they loved the ideas. The notion of starting with their current skills and habit patterns made a lot of sense; there were audible sighs of relief and a few "Thank God"s when I briefed them. It kicked off another round of Vernon-trauma sharing that I had to curtail quickly.

Unfortunately, the principles in the memo remained just that - things written on paper. I couldn't find a practical way to use them; they didn't make the day-to-day difference that I wanted. This weighed on me.

This particular meeting started with an update on a conversation I'd had with Martha the day before. "By the way, Bill, I don't have good news on the layoff front. The management team is still keeping it open as an option, and there's some new pressure from the board on Nick to implement the consultants' report. Your being away didn't help things much in your case. I don't think it hurt, but..."

"Don't tell me. The Anna Effect. Out of sight, out of a job, right?" She started to protest, but I cut her off, "It's okay, Martha. When I was away I had a change of heart."

That caught her by surprise, so I raised my hand quickly to quell her fear, gently patting the air in an "It's okay" gesture. The fact was, her job was probably riding on the success of the Alpha and Beta teams, and she didn't want to stop any of the progress. "I made a decision before coming back -- to do the very best work possible and let the chips fall where they may. When I was at RingCORE, I discovered a passion for coming up with ways for people to improve their personal time management methods; it's something I want to work on with my new team while I can. As for being laid off, I am going to do my best to not let the concern stop me from doing the right thing. Not just once, but over and over again. I didn't do enough of that in the past, but I'm over it. If I get laid off, I don't care, as long as I'm doing the right thing."

This came out with a strident tone that was completely unintended. I felt thrilled and alarmed. *Who said that?*

Her eyes opened wide and her face looked stunned. She tried to speak, but nothing came out.

I raised my hand as if I were in grade-school and asked in a Lizzy-esque tone, "Do-overs?"

In the middle of her laughing, she asked "Are you for real?" She recovered her senses and said "But you need to be realistic."

"You bet," I said a bit flippantly, but in that moment I realized that I'd need to be there for her, Sandy, my team and everyone else whose wellbeing was riding on the success of my little Beta experiment. This wasn't just about me; I knew that keep-my-job-at-all-costs thinking would kill it all.

By the time I got back to the team with Martha's warning, the rumor had already hit. Individual names of team members were mentioned. Debi called us the "Bad News Bears of Syscon".... the rejects. Ted labeled us the "Wretched Refuse," stealing a line from the bottom of the Statue of Liberty a few miles away. In the face of all the scary news, we laughed.

I called an end to the meeting before suggesting that we get together again the following day, because we weren't getting anywhere. Everyone agreed.

After lunch, Martha came to visit, and I showed her around our workspace. On the wall hung a huge poster with our team's mission statement alongside our project plan, which laid out a number of key milestones. To help remind us to give quality feedback, I placed a list of the steps we needed to follow, taken straight from my RingCORE experience. She murmured, "This is pretty challenging."

Each of our team members had a page on the wall with a list of our major deliverables, above the feedback skill that we were individually trying to improve. I explained to her that the effect of this "personal page" was interesting - we each knew what we wanted to improve and had to accomplish. "It was Kumar's idea to make them public, and it works like a charm. It shows us the progress we are making in this particular skill."

What I didn't tell her was that we needed something like this to focus our attention, because it was just too depressing to focus on our individual survival. Instead, we found it both challenging and interesting to have charts on the wall to help us use these new ideas.

Before she left, the team sat down with Martha to ask a few questions about the management team's plans to save the company.

"There's some information we need," Ted suggested, "to be successful. Is there a real future in using Zebon-style gamification at Syscon? Is the company serious about using it in future products? Is the Beta team important in the grand scheme of things?"

In his typical, blunt fashion, he finally asked, "Did Syscon just put us together in order to get rid of us as a group when the time is right?"

Martha spoke and said a bunch of words, but it was clear that she didn't have an answer.

* * *

A week later, my BP rang just as Sandy and I were stirring. It was a summery Saturday morning, and we could hear Lizzy playing in the living room as the sun sent its first bright rays into our bedroom. We had been up for about an hour, dozing off and on, enjoying each other's company.

Should we get to the farmer's market before breakfast, or after? It seemed to be an important decision at the time.

I answered my cell after seeing that it was my mother. Was she calling by mistake, as she sometimes did, after pressing a few wrong buttons?

"Bill, Honey, your father isn't well." Her voice was strained in a way that I didn't recognize.

"What's happened?" I immediately sat up as Sandy touched me on the arm. She propped herself up on one side, looking at me. There was no answer at first, then the sound of my Mom softly sobbing. She was mumbling so I could only hear "Robert Wood Johnson Hospital".... "Emergency Room"... "Your Dad." As a numbing, deadening feeling made its way through my body like an anesthetic, I found the presence of mind to say, "I'll meet you there as soon as I can."

"Okay, hurry. He's sick but I don't know how bad." Her voice filled with emotion, even as I went completely numb.

"Dad's in the hospital again," I explained to Sandy as I jumped out of bed and threw on some clothes.

As I backed the car out, I told myself to be careful. Accidents often happened at moments like this. As I passed joggers and kids cycling, I wondered how other people's lives could simply go on while my Dad's lay in the balance.

About ten minutes later, I pulled into the hospital's parking lot and made my way to Patient Information.

At the front desk sat a woman with a bright nametag that read, "Leslie-Ann." I waited impatiently for her to get off the phone. She had an island accent with a voice that lilted gently up and down. She told me that Mr. Crossley was still in the Emergency Room. With a fresh visitor's badge, I made my way through big double doors and winced at the cleaning-stuff smell of hospitals that always took me right back to my first visit —age 9 – when I had needed stitches for a long forehead gash earned on the playground.

Mom was sitting in the waiting area, looking pale. "He's had another stroke, but this time they say it's serious. They're looking at him right now." Her voice was shaking, tightened by an effort to hold things together, and her face was wan and tired. Out of nowhere, she had become a frail old person... *When did that happen?*

I hugged her wordlessly, and she held on to me, not wanting to let go.

About an hour later Dr. Andrews appeared. He had treated my father a few years ago when he had his first bout with TIA. He walked up slowly, and I could feel my mother's breath quicken as her hand fasten onto my arm. He sat down beside us.

"Your husband is out of immediate danger. He's pretty stable, but he did have another stroke that left him paralyzed on the right side. It's going to remain that way for some time, but the important thing now is to prevent the damage from spreading and another stroke from taking place."

Mom and I sat there quietly. She was usually the life of every party and one of the most talkative people I knew. Now, she was silent and probably very scared. My throat was dry.

Hearing the silence, he continued. "We'll need to keep him here for at least a week to help him recover his strength before we can assess him for permanent damage." My mother asked some questions, but I barely heard them.

I zoned out completely, maybe because he'd used the word "permanent." This could be the beginning of my Dad's end; the thought made me swallow and cough as my fingers started to tremble so hard that I had to grip my knees to steady them. When he finally walked away, we sat there, holding each other's hands without a word for what must have been a few minutes. I finally said to my Mom, "C'mon, I'll take you home."

# Chapter 13

On Monday morning, I made my way down to the cafeteria for a cup of coffee before starting work. Needing something strong, I took it black for a change to get my head out of the funk it was in. August mornings used to be my favorites.

The rest of the weekend had passed by in a blur. Instead of getting better, Dad had declined slightly, which had alarmed Dr. Andrews. He was transferred to intensive care, where they could keep a closer eye on him on Sunday night, and we were warned that the next few days were going to be critical. We were now looking at maybe ten days of touch-and-go treatment.

I hadn't even thought about work during the entire weekend; it felt as if my regular life had vanished on Saturday morning at the moment I got Mom's call. I was looking forward to returning to it, I thought.

As I sat staring out the window at the hills and back at my cup, I heard Martha's voice say very gently, "Bill, can I join you?"

She patted my shoulder as she took a seat beside me.

"I'm so sorry about your Dad -- what's the latest news?" Her voice was filled with care.

"He's not getting better anytime soon, I'm afraid. The doctors predict a slow recovery." The words came out of my mouth, but something about the warmth of her voice made me feel weak in the knees. My throat tightened and I choked out the word "recovery."

She gripped my arm, and I felt just a bit more stable. My mind flashed to the Beta team and made me wonder how I'd be able to lead the mid-morning meeting in this state. Everything in me wanted to head to the hospital where Mom was probably waiting with Sandy to find out when she could see my Dad.

Martha noticed me drift off. "You obviously have a lot on your mind, but I do have some good news that we have to handle quickly." She paused to make sure I was fully with her. I wasn't, but I pretended to be all there with as much strength as I could muster.

"The Beta team's work is moving to the center stage of the entire project." That helped to wake me up.

"It gets better. Manuel wants to use the project to show how good we are at educational gaming, so your feature set will be its major selling point."

This was surprising, as the work we had been doing had been a bit peripheral. We had positioned it as something for the future, but certainly not for the short term.

"And then here's the best of all. Your team needs to make a major presentation in a month's time to five potential customers. What's exciting is that they are all Fortune 50 companies. We have started to get a lot of interest among the big boys by applying the ideas related to gaming."

The news was almost good enough to make me forget what was happening at the hospital. "Wow -- I knew this would take off, but I had no idea it would happen so quickly."

"Well, the future is taking place right now, and your team has got to be ready for it."

I nodded but said nothing. Neither did Martha for a while. I let the news sink in. *What did this mean?* I was so tired that I couldn't even think through all of the options. I instantly knew that I wasn't the right person to lead the Beta team into a major presentation like this, on short notice. The team needed extra time, not less, which meant that I needed to focus my attention on getting my family through its current crisis.

"I'm not the right person," I concluded. "I was thinking about taking time off to take care of my Dad," I confided.

She didn't respond right away. "This is an awful situation. You have to keep your team going at an even higher level than before. The company is looking at four times as much revenue from gaming technology in the next fiscal year, and we're betting on your team and this presentation to get the job done. I know that you are reeling from the bad news this weekend, but I don't want you to underestimate what I'm saying."

"You mean, do it or else?" I was blunt. My Dad was suffering in the hospital, and I didn't have time to beat around the bush.

Her eyebrows rose, and she appeared shocked at my candor. But she answered bluntly also, "Yes. That's my advice, and I wish I didn't believe it. I wish it weren't happening now."

I was stunned and couldn't find a response. She looked at her watch. "I have to run. By the way, we just got a directive to stop using outside consultants until further notice. The division is freezing all non-essential costs to save expenses, so you need to find at least 5% of your budget to cut, because you'll probably be asked to give it up soon."

She gave me an apologetic look and left the empty cafeteria as I stared back to the hills. I needed to find a solution right away.

* * *

My Saturn climbed and curved through the hills of Bedminster on its way to nowhere in particular. So far, it was working - my head was clearing out as I'd hoped. An hour after the meeting with Martha, I still hadn't done more than let it all soak in.

How in the world was I supposed to pull this off? My instincts were telling me to do what I'd done in the past – simply steal time away from other parts of my life before assigning it to the problem at hand. It had worked back in college, when I almost flunked out one semester and needed to buckle down to save my skin. The ten pounds I lost in that episode, plus the dehydration and exhaustion... they were prices that I vowed I would never pay again.

*How could I create more time?*

I shook my head. *You can't create time.* That was the same stupid thinking that got everyone in trouble. After all, we only get a fixed number of hours per week, regardless of how much we are paid, what we work on, or who in the family is sick.

The problem I had now was that I had too many time demands to handle, putting me officially in the overload zone. The famous clip of Lucille Ball from the I Love Lucy Show on the out-of-control assembly line played across my mind, and I smiled as I coasted past local towns, valleys and crests.

Obviously, my mind had no problem creating too many time demands, and I didn't want to stop it from doing so, either. The meeting this morning with Martha would trigger an explosion of new ones.

The hard part was Emptying – sorting them out after they were created. Whenever that critical step didn't happen, I'd suddenly fail to enter the flow state and my productivity would fall.

On the last few calls with Andre and G, we had talked about some of this. "Sorting out" was necessary to prevent time demand overload, making Emptying the most important of the 7 Fundamentals. It was the point at which critical decisions were made that impacted each and every time demand.

Like many other experienced professionals, I had no problem with Capturing. We agreed that this skill was relatively easy to learn, even though email, voicemail, and Facebook walls had made it more challenging.

Emptying was about to become an even bigger headache for me as the theory we discussed on Sunday night was on the verge of turning into an awful reality. Based on our calls, I would need an urgent upgrade. The sooner the better.

It was weird, we realized - the habits that I used today could easily become obstacles tomorrow. G compared it to shoveling snow. Useful for small amounts of the stuff, but awful for huge snow drifts. Rushing to pick up the shovel right after it stops snowing can be an unproductive habit – sometimes, you just have to pick up the phone.

Andre jumped in with an example of his own. In the past couple of years, he was forced to unlearn the habit of constantly checking his email Inbox. Just as I had tried to explain to Vernon, the research backed up his experience.

So, I knew that I needed something new. But what? I still couldn't see how I could manage the new time demands coming at me from several directions at once.

With a growing feeling of exasperation, I pulled my car over at one of the scenic overlooks and dialed G's number. He picked up on the third ring, and I jumped in after his greeting.

"G, I need some help. In the last couple of days, I discovered a whole new bunch of time demands flying at me that I don't know how to handle." I told him all about my Dad's condition and what I had just learned from Martha.

"There's something you also need to know. Some consultants did a study that showed that there are too many Project Managers here at Syscon. As a result, I'm under the gun to show some major improvements."

He listened without interrupting, so quietly that I started to wonder if he was about to question my membership on our Sunday night team. Was I the weak link that needed to be replaced?

"I had no idea of these latest developments. As a team leader on a critical project, the stakes are high."

"Tell me about it... I thought I could help with the stuff that the three of us came up with. Now, I need to save my team and myself." On that last word, I heard my voice crack with fear and stress.

He paused for just a beat and announced, "You need another upgrade."

"Huh?"

"Your current habit patterns simply don't have the capacity to get all these time demands completed. You can either accept the situation as the status quo or do some work to get to the next level. Fortunately, the ladder that you put together is just the tool that we need to get you to the point where you can handle more time demands effectively without a stress increase."

I didn't wait to respond, "That sounds great, but how do I make that happen? I know how hard it is to change habits, especially when they don't involve a new BrainPhone." We both laughed. He repeated a Jamaican proverb he had taught us, "Tek serious ting mek joke," which means, "Take a serious matter and turn it into a joke." Then, he was back to business.

"I have been looking into this problem for a few months. Quite a few books have recently been released on the science of habit. We talked about *Blink* by Malcolm Gladwell on one of our calls. Have you run into *Change Anything* by the guys who wrote *Crucial Conversations*?"

"No, but what does that have to do with upgrading my productivity?"

"Well, so far, the 7 Ladders thinking tells us what we need to change and that we need to make small steps. But these books and other research tell us that we don't know how to change even when we know what needs to change. Think about smoking or losing weight. Everyone knows what to do, but that knowledge makes little or no difference."

"Well, yeah, that's true. But I learned some bad habits in zero time when I got my new BrainPhone."

"Yes, we all do. Even when we promise our wives that we won't." My BrainPhone failures were a constant source of amusement on our calls.

"There is a clue there," he continued, "We human beings respond well to some external stimuli, like a vibrating BrainPhone, and when a stimulus is repeated often enough, it helps us form habits. It happens *to* us rather than working *for* us. These books make the same point in different way. Time management mastery is a matter of creating the right external environment that will force us to develop the right habits... consciously." He emphasized that last word to make the point.

"How can I use that right now?" I asked. "I need something I can use, not just think about, at this point."

"I don't have that for you yet, my friend. Maybe in a month or two I will."

"G, I'm sorry, but I can't wait that long. I don't have it." I didn't know where telling him the truth would take me, but I felt bold and desperate enough to demand more.

"Okay, okay... let's talk again tomorrow. I'll try to get something together that you can use. Is it alright to call Andre in on this?" After I consented, he hung up.

As I placed my BP back in its holster, it rang. "Vernon."

His glassy stare from the meeting in Martha's office flashed into my mind.

"Hi Bill, have you heard the news about the Beta team?"

"Yes, it's come as a surprise to be honest. That presentation sounds like a big..." He cut me off.

"I think that you should report to me from this point on, given how important gaming is to Syscon's future; I should head up both the main project and this team. It would give us some additional assurance that you guys remain on track."

His words were all about helping the situation by doing the right thing, but I didn't believe him for a minute.

"I don't think that's a good idea," I said weakly.

"I do," he countered, rising irritation in his voice. "You guys need to hit the mark with that presentation, and I know that getting everyone back to the Master Time Method -- doing the right thing in the single best way -- is our only hope."

"Actually, we are getting help on improving our time management. We are each working on our personal plans to improve our skills and focusing on getting better during the course of this project. We're already helping each other make faster improvements than ever before."

"Well," he sneered, "as I'm sure you know, Xavier Kripanali says that no other systems are as well-designed as the Master Time Method, and it's not missing a single thing. I don't know what you could have found at RingCORE except a watered-down version."

The muscles in my neck tightened, and the car suddenly felt stiflingly hot. I spat back, "You are wrong. Each person is different, and they are all at different places. Ted started off well behind Kumar, for example. Telling them that they both need to read the same book and implement what it says doesn't work. They need something custom built. One-size-fits-all thinking won't work. It didn't work for me, and it won't work for the team. This isn't about one single method; it's about being a productive team, built on productive individuals. We're going to help each other get better, and that will make us successful. I'd appreciate it if you didn't interfere. Just allow me to lead this team the best way I know how."

I paused, but for a change, he had nothing to say. Neither did I - honestly, I didn't know how to accomplish this.

"I think we should talk to Martha about this," he suggested.

I almost shouted, "I don't have time for that. I'm leading this team and making it a better one. You can go talk to Martha and the other executives and try to talk them into doing whatever. I'm either in charge or not, but not halfway."

"No need to get upset, Bill, this isn't an emotional thing."

"Damned wrong. It's that and more."

With that, I hung up and screeched onto the road with my tires spinning.

* * *

"I have something for you."

I held my breath. When G spoke with that stronger-than-usual Caribbean accent in his voice, it paid to listen carefully.

"I have something for you. Check your Inbox – I just sent you some files to work with. I've been working on this stuff for some time, and it's not quite finished, but I think that you can start to use it now, under the circumstances."

My laptop downloaded the most recent email and I could see his message as well as a handful of attachments.

"The problem we have here is that you need to increase your capacity to handle time demands as quickly as possible without simply taking time away from one place to put in another. You have a demanding, busy life outside of the job and aren't willing to give it up to make this project work. Sound good so far?"

"Yes, that's right," I said, as I scanned the email message.

"My hypothesis is that the fastest, best way for you to get better is to involve everyone on your team in getting better. I believe that I have found a way to expand each person's individual performance with respect to dealing with time demands, and that would boost the team's ability to meet these challenging deadlines. Yes, I think I have a way."

*He'd better have something good.*

"Do you remember the call we had when you were in Phoenix? Andre wanted a way to teach people how to self-diagnose, build their own plans, and craft their own support systems. We tried to talk him out of it."

I remembered thinking that it was too much to ask for.

"Well, I think I can take each of your people through a diagnosis that shows them what their current level of skill in each fundamental happens to be. It will also help them figure out where they want to be in six months and how you can use each other to support the unique changes that need to be made. The good part is that these changes are visible and observable, so that you can help each other get better quite quickly."

I listened intently; I couldn't imagine all of this happening quickly enough to solve my pressing concerns. If he had to sit with each of us one at a time, it would take forever.

"Here's the real innovation," he continued. "I believe that I have figured out a way to train each of you, all together, in how to do this for yourselves. Teach you how to fish, in other words. The same things we talked about several weeks ago."

How could we possibly learn to do all that he described together with each other? And how long would it take? Feeling confused, I said nothing.

As if he'd heard my thoughts, he responded, "And all it would take is two days. Two days to teach each of you how to design and implement your own upgrades as you help each other realize them in your day-to-day work."

He went on to talk about the latest research in habit change and how teams had used several new techniques to make huge changes in performance, but the truth was that I was in no mood for theory. I absolutely loved the picture that was forming in my mind of each person being led by a personal improvement plan that was supported by the others. It echoed our efforts to improve our feedback skills using the charts on the wall of our office.

"How do we make sure we don't get overwhelmed?"

He said "As part of the training, you'd learn to focus realistically on one or two habit changes at a time. This, also, is supported by the research. The rest of the habits to be changed would be stretched out over time so that you can move smoothly from one to another.

"So, each person would be focused on a few habits at a time? Is that because we often fail when we try to implement behavior changes that are too big?"

"That's right. Add to that the fact that people usually have no idea where their current system is failing or succeeding, and you have a recipe for disaster."

"It sounds like you'd have to teach each of us how to make an upgrade and not just try to tell us which upgrade to make."

"Right. Everyone else out there tries to tell people exactly what to do. Instead, I suggest choices from a menu of skills, starting with their current level. No prescriptions. What each of you implements would be a small step from what you currently do. This would increase the odds of success."

"So, we'd end up going in the same direction at different speeds."

"Exactamundo -- one size doesn't fit all. Just like we talked about at RingCORE. I was inspired by a comment from my girlfriend about my oxtail stew. One day, we'll meet and you'll see that I have developed my own thing over the years. She asked me how I learned, and I told her that I started by following my mother's recipe. Then, as I learned the fundamentals of cooking, I changed it one step at a time and made it more suitable for me and my taste buds. Over time, I learned that knowing how to cook is more important than following a recipe."

I felt a sudden burst of inspiration, "That means that the ideal system fits your needs the best; it's the one that you come up with to suit your circumstances. It's perfectly crafted to fit all the dimensions of your life."

"Correctamente, amigo. And there are a lot of things it needs to fit... your current methods, your comfort with new technology, the number of time demands you must juggle each day..."

"... your family situation, company's expectations, corporate culture..."

"...even national culture. More, probably. Can you see what you'd have in the end? Each person with a custom plan."

"You bet! And the support we give each other would be laser-targeted at the skills we are working on."

"Also," G continued, "some evidence shows that people who are helping each other feel less time-pressured. You might want to take advantage of that -- I'll send you the article by Michael Horton."

"When there's a lofty goal at stake, people do more. I guess there's nothing loftier than helping someone else you work with."

"Correct!"

"G -- when can you come? Let's set up some dates for you to work with our team. Two days, you said?"

"Right, and I'll send along my invoice, too."

My heart jumped, skipping a beat. "Send me email with the proposed cost as soon as you can, will you?"

I hung up with a growing sense of alarm. Martha had been clear about not using outside consultants in order to cut spending. *I'm stuck.*

* * *

I forgot to turn my phone off, as I usually do on my lunch time power-walks, and, of course, it rang. The three-mile trail around Syscon's property was just about to bend the south corner and go upwards into the woods when I paused underneath a strong, silent elm.

"Mike -- it's been a long time!"

He got right to the point. "We are about to make an offer to a colleague of yours - Vernon Vaz. He applied for a manager's position working for me, and after the interviews, we liked him enough to call his references. They were all glowing, but none of them had worked closely with him, and before we make him an offer I decided to give you a call. Just wanted to make sure we are on track here... have you ever worked with him?"

Vernon? Going to RingCORE? I knew he wanted that promotion badly enough, but... RingCORE? Phrases like "oil and water" and "chalk and cheese" floated to my lips, but as I readied my reply, the call dropped. This often happened on this particular trail.

We were less than a week from the start of G's training, so this came as a bit of a distraction. All I wanted to focus on was whether or not G's training would work as planned, and I hadn't thought of or spoken with Vernon in weeks. Plus, I had negotiated a contract with G quietly, without telling Martha or Manuel.

This could get me fired, but with my back against the wall, I reasoned that it was better to be fired for doing the right thing than laid off because I was too afraid to try to make a difference. This was why I had come back to Syscon.

The phone rang again, and I pressed it to my ear without looking at the Caller-ID. "Mike, I don't know about that. About Vernon, I mean."

I paused, because all I could make out was his breathing on the other end. "Mike, can you hear me?"

Then, once again, the call dropped. I looked down at the phone, and there was the caller's name: "Vernon Vaz." *Oh cripes.*

In the next instant, the phone rang again and this time I took a long moment to stare at Caller ID before answering. It announced, "Mike Springer."

"Looks like we just got cut off. As I was saying, we are about to make Vernon an offer, but after talking with him a few minutes ago, something told me to call you before pulling the trigger."

"I don't think it's a good idea," I exclaimed, exhaling as I spoke. "Here's why."

Speaking bluntly, I told him the truth of my experience working with Vernon and why I didn't think he was a good fit for RingCORE. I made it clear that there was a tremendous gap between their culture and his style.

I concluded by admitting, "I could be wrong here. This is just my experience. He might be a different person in a new environment."

"But you wouldn't bet on it, would you?"

"Hell no."

He thanked me and we closed out the conversation.

*Oh well.* Vernon was probably trying to call me to give me a heads up about Mike calling. And now he knew. The freeze at Syscon meant that his goal of being promoted wouldn't happen here.

A few minutes later my phone rang again.

"Vernon Vaz."

This time, I ignored it. He'd find out soon enough that I had just blocked his cherished promotion at RingCORE.

* * *

A couple of days later, Mike called me back and once again, got straight to the point.

"So much for Mr. Vernon Vaz. Thank God I spoke with you. So, Andre and I were talking," he explained, "and we want to give you a fresh opportunity. The truth is, you are the one we really want for this manager's job. We just didn't think you'd take it. But this stuff is heating up, and we want to try to convince you again."

"Look Mike, our project is..." but he cut me off.

"Don't say no yet. There's more. This job is going to be funded by a client who desperately needs the Zebon technology. We are prepared to help make it worth your while with a $30,000 signing bonus, along with a bunch of other perks that Syscon isn't in a position to match."

"Whooooaaaaa... Nelly," I whispered.

"Right," he responded. "I won't take an answer from you now, but we are delaying another candidate for a few weeks until you can sort yourself out and give us a final answer. It's something we haven't done in a long time, so bear that in mind. What Andre wants, Andre gets, and right now... Tag, you're it. Until the clock stops at the end of September. By then, we must have an answer."

"September," I repeated, searching for a response. All I could croak out was "Thanks."

# Chapter 14

Vernon stood at the doorway to Martha's office looking annoyed. "Where's Martha? We're supposed to be meeting now." He was pissed.

There was no one else in her office - just me - and his rhetorical question filled the room with a quiet chill. It didn't stop him from sitting down and opening up his smartphone without saying a word to me. Martha's email must have rattled him a bit. The lost job at RingCORE probably made him think that I was the cause.

```
==========================
```
**Martha. Adelman**
```
------------------------------------------------
```
From: Martha.Adelman@syscon.com
To: Bill.Crossley@syscon.com, BetaTeam@syscon.com
CC: Vernon.Vaz@syscon.com, Manuel.Bonares@syscon.com
Subject: Great job by the Beta Team.

Thanks for the great job you guys did on the Fortune 50 meeting. They were impressed, and it's set the stage for an important addition to Syscon's product line. The marketing guys want to meet, as you can imagine.

I know this took hard work and some sacrifices.
```
------------------------------------------------
```

She was right about the sacrifices. I sat in her office in complete silence, with only the sound of Vernon tapping away at his smartphone. With nothing else to do, I looked back at the events of the past two months, ever since Mike offered me a job at RingCORE.

I could afford to sit back and rest a bit. My Dad was still causing us some sleepless nights due to his ups and downs, but he was home from the hospital and slowly recovering.

The Beta Team was still in overdrive following the workshop with G. As soon as it was over, everything gained a new level of intensity: every meeting, every deliverable, every conversation. Working hard while improving our habits was easier than I had feared once we all had clear heads. It was, however, taxing; it reminded me of my RingCORE days.

The team was soon running ahead of the original schedule, and the company was starting to notice. It inspired some rumors about our cutting corners, which annoyed the heck out of me, but I ignored them while secretly hoping that Martha, Manuel and others were paying attention to the true story. So far, the word about my spending some of our budget to bring G in hadn't leaked out. The retreat with him was held at an off-site lodge after the team was sworn to secrecy. They were happy to be part of a juicy conspiracy.

The two big things G gave us were paying off. Each person on the team had learned how to manage their own upgrade, just as he had intended. The timing couldn't have been better, as we all needed to make some critical changes. The need for these changes was obvious from the diagnosis he encouraged us to repeat every few months. Every day, we'd talk about how much the new improvements helped us with non-work-related things – time with our families, communities, churches, exercise programs, etc. Comments from people in these areas started to trickle back in. They became such a consistent theme that we created a wall with some of their quotes. We labeled it the "Impact Wall," and it included feedback from both work and personal lives.

The second big thing he gave us was the valuable coaching from our teammates. Once we understood that "habits change slowly" and "knowing what to change is only the beginning," it wasn't hard to see that we could help each other deliver the upgrades we needed. He promised that we would be able to realize them in our lives just "a bit faster." He was wrong about that. It was happening a LOT faster.

In fact, having the support of other team members made these changes happen at a dizzying pace, and I was excited to see them happen for me too. There was no question of smartphone abuse on my part. My team members were vigilant to the point of aggression - I could not use my BrainPhone in inappropriate ways around them. Practicing the new habit of leaving it untouched in meetings became easy.

Time demands were flowing through our team like a strong river, and we were getting to the point where it didn't matter who was assigned to which ones - we were all becoming responsible for the successful disposal of every task.

Inside, I smiled at the memory of the Sunday calls with Andre and G, where this was all dreamt up. G kept adding more new stuff based on the most recent research, so we always needed to keep current. Unfortunately, our three-way calls with Andre were on a month-long hiatus (he was on business in the Far East), but we kept him in the loop via email. On our last call, he had asked G when he'd be ready to train all of RingCORE, and they were starting to look at time frames.

"Damn it, I have things to do." Once again, Vernon spoke to the empty room, not really expecting me to answer. Only the sound of the a/c unit broke the silence with its quiet and faithful hum. Mike eventually confirmed they had offered him only a lateral move: another project manager role, which he promptly turned down.

A conversation with Ted flashed into my mind. Earlier that week, he'd caught me on the way out to my car after a typically hard day.

"That skinny-ass idiot has been bad-mouthing our team around the company! You need to do something. Three people have come to me in the past week to give me the heads-up -- Vernon's telling people that we are spending huge amounts on outside consultants."

Before I could dwell too much on that piece of news, Martha entered the office, followed by Manuel.

She seemed to notice the silent antagonism. She shot me a surprised look. I took that to mean that she didn't know that Vernon and I were at odds with each other. She made a nervous little joke, which only left me wondering what to expect and why Manuel was in the meeting. This was no ordinary update.

"How's the family, Bill?" she asked.

"Getting by... one day at a time." My voice crackled with my short, public reply, so different from our private conversations, which were warm, caring, and filled with light-hearted jokes. I regretted my short answer immediately, but didn't say anything more.

"Vernon, how are Stevie and Nell?"

I didn't notice his answer because her question rang a distant bell somewhere in my memory. Vernon's answer was overdone: a list of accomplishments at school, football games and ballet recitals. Pulling out my BrainPhone, I did a search in my messages for Stevie + Nell. Up popped that mysterious email from Stevnellie9612@aol.com.

My throat tightened and went dry.

"Stevnellie9612@aol.com." I said this aloud as soon as he finished and looked straight at Vernon. For a moment, his eyes looked panicked, and then they went deadly calm, like a winter day in February. *Anything and everything to win. While setting up people like me to lose.*

Manuel started, "Thanks for coming, guys. I wanted us to meet to clear the air about a few things about the Beta team. The team is doing quite well, but Vernon has raised enough concerns to make us think that we need to at least hear them out and then let Bill give us a few explanations about what he's doing. We don't have more than an hour to spend on this, because I have another meeting. Vernon, over to you."

My back stiffened and I rubbed my sweaty hands together, trying to dry them.

"Thanks, Manuel. Bill and his team have been trying hard to meet their new mandate. They now have a technology that can revolutionize this company's future. I think that it's important that they succeed: and that's all I want... the company's success."

Martha and Manuel nodded their heads in agreement. I didn't.

"I think we should do what's right for the company and not for any individual person in the Beta Team." It was all classic office politics, and I could tell that he was building a case for something that I wouldn't like. I tried to hide my disgust.

It didn't work. Martha cut in after glancing at me. "I think that's what we all want, isn't it?" As she said it, she looked at me rather pointedly. It took me a split second to respond to her lead, but in that small gap in time, something big happened.

My mind flashed back to the day I saw those posters at RingCORE, just before I started meeting regularly with Andre and G. Then it jumped to the commitment I'd made before returning to Syscon - set aside my personal fears and concerns while doing the right thing for the company that I cared more for than my own skin.

It was a strange moment. Things slowed down for a few seconds. I could sense an opportunity opening up, but also fear. It made me want to defend myself by running away to the safety of RingCORE.

"That's actually why I came back to Syscon."

It was a cryptic remark, to be sure, but it got Manuel's attention and Martha's eyes also opened wide. Vernon didn't notice one bit of it as he hurried on to try to get some points on the board. He wanted to win something today, I could tell.

"As you both know, before Bill left Syscon for his sabbatical, he was well on his way to implementing the Master Time Method as a standard technique. I think that your directives in this case were right on the money, Manuel, as it's just what we need around here."

I looked at Manuel and Martha, confused, deliberately revealing my surprise. Martha jumped in. "I don't know if it was a directive. Manuel has used it for years and thought it would be a good idea for everyone to have some exposure."

Manuel nodded. "Yes, it's the best system that's around. That's why I asked you to get everyone to use it."

Vernon took that as a show of support. "We all need to be using the same standard here at Syscon. The book says that there's no halfway measure. You either use the method correctly or not at all. Right Manuel?" Martha's boss nodded. "It does say that, yes." His body didn't convey a whole lot of enthusiasm, so Vernon reacted by trying to put him on the spot, "After all, I only got into the Master Time Method because of your influence and leadership on the Sunset Project and your long-time relationship with Xavier Kripanali."

The Sunset Project had ended just before I returned from Florida. It was a big success, but the MTM angle was new to me. So was the fact that Manuel had a "relationship" with its author, which added a hint of danger that made me shift uneasily. After an awkward silence with a cursory nod from Manuel, Vernon continued.

"The key to the Master Time Method is its simplicity; follow the rules of behavior that it lays out. Stick to them and don't stray from them. The guy who wrote the book is a certified genius. It's a whole system that works together as one, and it's a big mistake to think that pieces can be cherry-picked here and there. You just don't get to do that, but that's exactly what Bill has done in his memo. He wants us to do all this complicated stuff when there's no need."

He pulled out a copy of my 7 Ladders memo as well as the training manual that G had prepared for us. They were both heavily marked up in red ink. *How did he get those?* I stared in amazement at my private little memo, which had developed a life of its own. I had thought only a handful of training manuals were printed.

"Bill's theories would never work in actual practice. It's all a bunch of ideas with no meat. When someone picks up the Master Time Method, they know exactly what to do. Here, he's leaving it all open-ended and up to the individual to decide what to do. Most people are lazy and just want simple instructions. It's not practical and can't replace the Master Time Method -- although it has one or two ideas that Xavier Kripanali has already considered and discarded."

Martha and Manuel nodded in agreement. Every time he used the phrase "Master Time Method," I pictured my hands around his neck.

"It's crazy to think that everyone needs to understand, let alone implement, something this complicated."

They all looked at me, but I was still in a daze, lost in my thoughts. *Manuel was the real sponsor behind MTM? Did he get Vernon to send me that email?* I fumbled around for a response, and when I said nothing, he read from a photocopied page, "The Master Time Method is designed to maximize your productivity by limiting your choices about the right thing to do. It's important to follow the Master Time Method exactly as it's designed in order to be most productive. What's most important is to trust the system to work as it's meant to."

Manuel interrupted, "Get to your point, Vernon." He responded by holding up a finger and stating, "Xavier Kripanali says that he can't imagine anyone using a better system -- the Master Time Method is complete and needs no additions or refinements. That's what we should follow here at Syscon — we shouldn't run off making up our own stuff." He was looking straight at Manuel, who was actually nodding at this point.

It was time for me to say something. Everyone knew it, and once again, they turned to look at me. Befuddled, I started talking but what came out sounded like a whine. "I don't agree, Vernon..." I mumbled, but at that precise moment, Martha jumped in.

"Guys, I need a bathroom break. Can we get back together after five minutes?"

* * *

In the men's room, I stared at myself in the mirror then closed my eyes with a prayer. *Thank you, Martha.* I made sure to find a quiet bathroom far from her office where I could be alone.

Hot, dark-green feelings of contempt were bubbling inside me. Anger at Vernon for trying to use Manuel and Martha to beat down our ideas. What did he want the Beta team to do, turn the clock back and adopt his approach?

I ranted to the mirror, talking to myself quietly. My lips were moving with the stuff I wish I had said in the meeting a few minutes ago, when Martha's words came back to me. ...*what we all want*. I said to myself, this time out aloud: *What if we all want the same things?*

What if she was right? All three of us, on some level, were trying to reach the same objective. Vernon had some other agenda also, but I didn't have to be upset with his approach, or try to engage it with some clever put downs. If we wanted so many of the same things, then I should offer my best thinking. My best efforts to accomplish the goals we had in front of us. MTM was just another alternative.

Ted once asked me a Zen riddle. "If you offer someone a gift and he declines to accept it, to whom does the gift belong?" After I looked at him rather stupidly, he replied with a grin, "The answer is up to you."

When I walked in, Vernon was writing furiously on Martha's whiteboard. He wrote two lists before sitting down. One was headed up by the letters MTM. Under it was a list of benefits: "available" / "accepted" / "easy to understand" / "standard" / "expert." The other list was headed by the words "7 Ladders." That list was empty. It was an open invitation to a head-to-head battle.

Martha resumed the conversation, "Bill, what do you think of what Vernon said before our break?"

I took a breath before I started. "I agree with most of it. MTM is a great book that outlines a fantastic system. If this were only about following someones pattern of behavior, we'd be in good shape, because Xavier Kripanali is a very smart guy."

I paused and took another breath. Clean, cool fresh air always seemed to clear my head, although Martha's small office was making its usual swing from chilling cold to stuffy heat.

"However, the world we live in today is too demanding. I bought a BrainPhone thinking that it would help be more productive, but it mainly made things worse in terms of my time management, at least at first. My Dad fell sick at the start of the Beta project, and I had to scramble to adjust my methods to keep my head above water. The big thing I learned is that it's better to know how to upgrade your time management system when you need to than it is to have the right one for the moment."

Manuel looked puzzled. "What do you mean, for the moment?"

"I remember when I first learned the practices outlined in MTM. It was great for that time of my life. It made a big difference. However, when I was in Florida, the high-pressure circumstances forced me to make some changes that went against the book, but made me more productive. The biggest one was that I started using a single schedule instead of multiple to-do lists."

It was as if I planted a light in Manuel's eyes, which lit up like one of those sparklers I used to play with as a kid. "Really?" he said with a voice full of enthusiasm. "Me too."

Vernon's eyes were also blazing, but in quite a different way. I looked away, deciding not to focus on him at all for the rest of the conversation, if I could help it.

Martha summed it up, "It's the old teach-a-man-to-fish thing."

"Exactly. In fact, it was amazing to discover in our workshop that we each had invented our own system between the ages of 18 and 25, but had partially forgotten it. We were actually relearning a lost skill." They all seemed to agree so I didn't linger.

"As individuals, when we diagnosed our current systems, we discovered that we had each been doing a pretty good job under the circumstances."

"Diagnosis? How did you do that?" This was Vernon, who appeared grudgingly interested.

"The materials we used were provided by G, a time management innovator. He did a great job building on the ideas in the 7 Ladder memo and went several steps further. He took my notes outlining a few skills at each belt level and came up with complete definitions – it looks very different from what I originally wrote. He sent us seven mini-questionnaires that we used to grade our skills in each fundamental. In the memo, I discussed the way people develop uneven skills because we're self-taught -- do you recall?"

All the heads were nodding.

"Well, sure enough, among Beta Team members, our profiles of the 7 fundamentals were all over the place. It was remarkable. Only those of us who had tried hard to implement MTM before the project had similar profiles."

"That's interesting," started Martha. "My master's degree included some instructional design courses, and one of the things we talked about all the time was the different needs of adult learners. You need to start with the fact that they already have knowledge and skills to build on. It's a big difference to start with where they are now, rather than assuming that they know nothing at all."

"Right," I said. "Anyone can use this approach to improve, even if they've already worked with MTM." Vernon looked as if he wanted to pop, but I ignored him.

"I'm missing something -- what does this actually look like?" asked Martha. I took a minute to send my personal profile over to her laptop from my BrainPhone, and within a few minutes she had it up on her screen.

"It looks like a report card, with a score in each of the 7 areas," she said. "I can see the unevenness you talked about."

"Right, I have a green belt in Capturing, but only a yellow belt in Emptying. All of us who had MTM backgrounds had low belts in Scheduling." That final comment was for Vernon's benefit; I was messing with him now, but only a little.

"Once I completed my profile, any fool could see what I needed to improve. My team mates made this abundantly clear," I said, smiling at the memory. "I knew a lot of tips and tricks, but the team helped me see where I needed to apply them, the best sequence of improvement and the kind of help I'd need."


I thought for a moment and continued, "I say that this puts an end to the blame game. Let me repeat what I said before, but a bit differently. Because of our amnesia with regards to putting together our own system, we tend to approach books like MTM thinking that we don't know anything, or that we are blank slates. People make the mistake of putting their focus on what's in the book and try to follow it, without understanding where they are coming from in terms of their current habits. Not surprisingly, a large number of them fail because it's too far a distance to travel."

"Okay..." said Manuel, urging me to continue.

"Then they blame MTM for not working. Or, if they are successful, they think that it's the answer to everything. Some even become enforcers, thinking that the way to success is making other people stick to its rules." I looked at Vernon pointedly. I offered, "That's not all their fault. MTM places too much emphasis on compliance to an external standard." I paused to make sure that everyone was with me.

"The point is, G's materials put the responsibility for understanding and upgrading our time management methods right back in our laps. This was scary at first, and we complained that we couldn't possibly learn how to re-design something so complex. He insisted, and we persevered... and ended up loving the feeling of being in control. Rather than following someone else' system, we are taking charge of our own."

"Ohhhhhh," said Martha.
"Que bueno" whispered Manuel.
Vernon looked stunned.

"He showed us how to use the 7 Ladders to evaluate where we are now, where we want to be in the future, and how to close the gaps. He also added in a new piece that he's still working on... how to set up habit change supports that ensure that the upgrades stick and become permanent behavior changes."

"Was that easier to put in place because you were a team?" asked Manuel.

"Exactly. We provided a big chunk of support. There's no way we'd be ahead of our schedule if we didn't have each other. For example, Debi tried hard to remember everything she needed to do each day and seemed to be getting worse as the project became more complex. During our training, she identified the need to develop a habit of writing everything down in a safe place. At first, she failed miserably, but her teammates wouldn't allow it, not even once. After two weeks of their reminders, she hardly travels anywhere without a bright blue pad. We all benefited from her improvements."

"You have moved the focus away from following an external system, to following your own understanding, using your own goals, and crafting your own support." Manuel summarized beautifully. "And to think that I felt guilty for not following MTM exactly as it's laid out." He shook his head vigorously as we all laughed.

"This sounds like a combination of some of the best practices that exist in behaviour change. This approach hits all the nails on the head. People want to be self-directed when it comes to their learning, and trying to force them to follow a foreign set of practices just doesn't work. I think that's why MTM hasn't been more successful. It's very old-school thinking -- just tell people what to change, and they should be able to make it happen. That doesn't work in complex disciplines like time management."

Vernon looked ready to explode, but he didn't say anything at all.

Manuel continued, "But isn't it true that MTM is easier to understand? In that approach and almost every other one I am aware of, you just tell people what they should be doing. They don't have to figure anything out. What if people aren't smart enough to do what you guys have done? That could be a major obstacle to implementation on a larger scale."

Vernon came alive suddenly, "That's right. It's not realistic to think that people have what it takes to do their own designing. This hasn't been tested. It's only been done once, while millions of people have implemented the Master Time Method around the world. This new approach is way too hard – it requires too much from the average person. It won't work."

Manuel nodded. "I see a major obstacle here," he said slowly with his heavy Mexican accent. "Plus, we are talking about long implementation times. MTM only requires a day of training. This takes much longer to work."

My temper started to rise with a host of answers to Manuel's objections. He was wrong, but before I could tell him why, Martha chipped in quickly, "How many weeks has it been since your team completed that training?"

"Seven or eight weeks," I replied.

"And you are already seeing the changes you described?"

"Absolutely. It's the reason we are ahead."

"Good, because we only have ten minutes left in our meeting and I need to give you some news. We thought the Beta team would wrap up in the March to April time-frame. Now, your fame precedes you. Nick heard about your progress and the Fortune 50 meeting. He needs you to wrap up by the end of December. At that point, you must present your recommendations and findings along with a product ready for the marketing department to take on the road. That gives you ten to twelve weeks to have a working prototype ready."

I had to stifle the curses that flew into my mind. Martha, Manuel and Vernon looked at me for a response, but I wasn't about to say them out aloud. That anger simply could not come out now, fueled by the fear of being laid off that I had suffered with for more than a year. My palms, which were sweaty from Manuel's doubts and Vernon's attacks, formed into fists. The memory of that secret email hadn't faded a bit, and I wanted some revenge.

As I put my frustrated feelings into words, there was a knock on the door, and one of the department's secretaries poked her face in. "Bill..." she said as her hand motioned towards me. "Your wife has been trying to reach you all morning. Can you call her immediately?"

I excused myself from the meeting and picked up the phone: Sandy. The static on the phone was awful. "Bill... had a relapse. You need to head to your parents' home... going down fast."

"I'm going there now." I almost shouted in the phone to make sure she got the message.

I looked from the secretarial pool towards the direction of the meeting room, and I asked someone to let Martha know that I'd be heading out to handle a personal emergency. I made a bee-line to my car.

* * *

My Saturn raced out of the parking lot towards the ramp to the highway. Back roads were an option, but this was the fastest route for a mid-morning dash. Once again, it was weird that no one in the other cars seemed to care that my father had just taken a turn for the worse.

Four days ago, he had returned home from yet another trip to the hospital, looking wobbly but insisting that he didn't need any help. I got all choked up watching him struggle for balance like a baby - so different from my childhood memories of my dad: a big, strong man.

As I got on the highway, I wondered - Did he fall down? Was it another stroke? What did he need to get better, and whom did he need it from?

*If he's that bad, I'd better make this count.*

When I pulled up to the house, I saw the answer to one question. An ambulance with flashing lights was pulled up in front of my parents' home and emergency personnel were wheeling my father out on a gurney. I parked the car in the middle of the road and ran up to see him just before he was placed in the back of the vehicle.

But the hair was dark, and my heart collapsed when I realized why. It wasn't my father at all, but my dear, precious mother. Her face was pale and covered with a breathing mask of some kind. She wasn't moving.

My knees weakened as my eyes filled; I called out her name, but the EMT's directed me back towards the house. I stood there as they drove off, stunned and unable to move. The traffic kept passing along the road long after the lights disappeared around the block.

172

*Where was Dad?*

Flinging doors open, I found him lying on the hospital bed set up in the living room. He was sitting up and called out, "Bill! I'm over here."

I rushed over and held his arm. His face was concerned, but clear.

"Your mother," he whispered. "She went to fetch some tea from the pantry when I heard her fall -- a bang on the cupboard. I called her, but nothing. So I called Mrs. Adewumi from next door and she came right over to call Sandy. Is she okay? What are you going to do?"

"I'm going to the hospital to find out, Dad -- keep your phone near." Only then did I notice that we weren't alone. Mrs. Adewumi was sitting quietly, listening.

"Don't worry Bill, I'll take care of things here for a couple of hours," she offered.

"Thank you," I almost shouted in gratitude as I made my way to the car before returning to the highway.

Within a couple of hours, I got some answers. My dear mother, who had never been in the best of health, had suffered a seizure. While falling, her hip had fractured. Now, she needed emergency surgery to repair the broken bone, and it needed to happen that night. I immediately called my Dad and Sandy with the news; they both sounded relieved but very worried. At least she was alive, and something was being done about the problem right away. Maybe if everything went well, she'd make a full recovery.

It wasn't long, however, before I started worrying about what this meant in the next few months. Obviously, my mother was going to need help, and a lot of it. Her full-time job had recently consisted of taking care of my father, and now she needed someone to take care of her. How would that play out?

The following morning, I saw her. She looked frightened but relieved. Inside, I was scared. *She's never looked anything like this.* Wearing a white hospital smock, she appeared so weak that she seemed glued to the bed. Only the right side of her body was freely moving, just as the doctor had warned.

"Billy, are you going to be able to take care of us? I don't want anyone else to be around bothering us. It's got to be you."

She was right, and I knew it. No one could play the role of caregiver the way I could. Once, when I was about fifteen, they both came down with a bad case of chicken pox. Confined to bed, I turned into a young Marcus Welby, M.D., making them think for years that I'd be a doctor someday.

"Not to worry, Mom, I'm going to be with you guys all the way back to good health and I'm going to take time from work to do it."

But I was no longer fifteen. Yesterday in the Beta meeting, a ton of new time demands had been scrunched into a few short weeks. As I looked at her, I tried not to panic. Syscon didn't care about your personal problems - the lack of an employee health plan or family leave program bore evidence of that. The last employee to get really sick, a receptionist, was simply let go after a month.

"Billy... it's important to keep on doing a great job at your work. I always wanted to cause a big difference and you kids were my way. You have got to do the same thing in your life. While you have time."

*Was she being profound,* I wondered, *or just babbling?* Then I recalled a phrase she picked up from a personal development class she took back when I was about ten. "Cause a big difference" sounded a lot like the phrase that RingCORE often used.

After that weekend, that's all she could talk about for a year - how to "cause a big difference." A few years had passed since she had last used the phrase, but it had stuck with her.

"Don't worry Mom. That's why I'm back at Syscon."

She looked at me with confused eyes, but closed them with a wince then sank back deep into the bed. Her breathing turned into a faint snore within a few minutes. I tried to wipe away tears, but they flowed freely at the sight of my Mom getting old, all of a sudden.

* * *

When I got up the next morning to use the bathroom, I hadn't slept all night. It was Saturday morning, and I had tossed around in bed until the clock registered 4:00 a.m. It was still dark outside, with no hint of pre-dawn light.

I lay back down, trying hard not to wake Sandy.

"When are you going to tell me everything?"

Her voice came out of the dark and startled me, just as I sat down on the bed. I lay my head on the pillow and turned slightly towards her. She was looking up at the ceiling, and I couldn't make out her face in the dark. She sounded hurt. I struggled to think of a response and finally grunted out a question, "What do you mean?"

She shot back, "I feel as if you've been holding back something and trying hard not to spill the beans about... something big. I have felt that way for months. Long before you went to RingCORE... but then, while you were there, it seemed to go away. Is there something happening at work? At Syscon? Or RingCORE?"

I lay back on the pillow, shocked. How had she guessed? I thought I had done my best to hide my situation. The burden of carrying the secret made me hate it all. Martha. Manuel. Syscon. Everything.

But not as much as I hated the darkness of a mid-afternoon bedroom and someone I loved being unable to summon the energy to even take a bath. Once again, I fought the helpless feeling that flashed across my mind. *Never again.* I lay in a frightened silence with Roma's words racing through my mind.

"Bill," she whispered, as if reading my mind, "we want the same thing and can get through this together. Trust me, I can take it. It would make a big difference if you'd let me know what's happening."

Swallowing, I latched on to her words - *Make a big difference.* My back relaxed, and I turned over on my side to face her.

"Syscon has been threatening to lay me off for some time. The buzz on the street has been that my name is on the list of those to be included in the next round of cuts. Martha has been encouraging me to find ways to be more productive so that my name doesn't appear on the list."

She said nothing for a full minute, then sat up and stared at me.

*Too blunt... explain.*

"That's why I have been working so hard on my time management skills -- too many things have fallen through the cracks. They were going to make me lose my job. I didn't tell you anything because I thought I could turn it around quickly, and I didn't want to make you worry. God forbid the kids get even a whiff of it."

Now, her face was getting red and her eyes filled.

"At RingCORE, I found out that I didn't even care about keeping the job as much as I did about making a difference in some way with the guys I work with -- Ted, Martha, Kumar -- everyone. I came up with a bunch of stuff myself and learned all sorts of new things that Syscon hadn't even discovered. My goal was to take it all back. So far, it's helped the Beta team, but they still want to get rid of Project Managers. And now, this stuff with Mom and Dad."

My voice cracked at the very end.

Sandy was wiping away tears, and that just got to me. A single, tired sob forced its way out and tears from my eyes overflowed onto my cheeks.

"I just wish you had told me. I knew something was going on, but I didn't know what it was, or what to do about it. Don't you think this is the kind of thing we should be working out together, rather than apart? It's awful to be on different pages, especially about stuff that's so important. All this time I could have been helping you... us... get through this. How about we put an end to doing this solo?"

"–Okay, I'm all for that. I don't want to do it alone, but it's the only way I know. There is so much at stake: our home, our lifestyle, your health. Remember what your doctor said?"

She almost jumped out of the sheets. "Are you talking about 'Mister' Roma? Well, I have some news for you. It looks like our dear family therapist forged a whole bunch of his credentials. No state license, no PhD, nothing. They released him from jail about a month ago, according to Tonia. Don't you think we should forget about him and his advice? Plus, that was a long time ago and... I'm not a weak victim. I'm your partner. I'm just so sure that we can do this together. I want to."

I stared at her. Roma was a quack? The last few months suddenly felt like a huge loss. Instead of helping, I had made things worse.

"I'm so sorry," I said slowly, as the full impact of my withdrawal over several months seeped in. "I desperately want your help.... I have always wanted it. Let's do what you said and start doing this together."

We hugged and lay back down with her head on my shoulder. We talked some more about the details of the last year: the list, Martha, Vernon, G, Andre... everything since my week in Shreveport. After an hour, we were finishing each other's sentences, and I felt happier than I ever had.

"But what do you need now, Honey? How can I help? With your parents sick and your Mom needing you near her, how can you continue to lead that project?"

"Well, there's more. Let me tell you about RingCORE." Her eyes opened wide when I got to the part about the 30 grand. She absorbed it all and said, "We'll have to decide about that -- but let's do it together. Whether you accept or not, you'll need to make sure that the Beta team succeeds."

I didn't have an answer, but she did. "How about working for half a day at a time until your parents' situation stabilizes. If you could make it over to their place by lunchtime each day, it would make a huge difference. Perhaps we could find someone to stay the night and the morning."

"Keep going," I said.

"Lizzy and Rebecca -- I can bring them over in the afternoon and we could all have dinner together at your parents' place. It would be a tricky schedule to keep, but if we work together, we'll have a good shot. Can your team be organized to work without you, so that you hit those new nine-week targets?"

When I told her about the habit support system we had in place, she smiled. "When can I get some of that first-class treatment?"

She was being coy, but I pressed her to say more. "It's just that these time demands from our family and home don't seem to be captured in a capture point in the same way. Your memory for that stuff sucks!"

I laughed as she absolutely murdered some of my favorite buzzwords.

"I obviously have been over-focusing on work. Can you help me make sure that I treat all time demands with equal importance?"

"Agreed! You should capture that somewhere and then go empty it later!"

I smiled, and instead of keeping my next worrying thought from her, I said it out aloud. "Now I have to find a way to get the Beta team to succeed without me. And I need to make damned sure that Vernon doesn't end up running the show."

\* \* \*

"Bill, don't kill the messenger here... but we have another change of date."

Martha raised her hands in frustration as she sat with me in my office the following morning. The sense of calm purpose that had entered me during the conversation with Sandy hadn't left, but now it was under attack. This never-ending game of "Whack-a-Mole" was getting tiring. Progress with Sandy. Then bad news from Martha.

"I'm so sorry to hear about your Mom. I can't imagine what this must be like."

I nodded. I could barely imagine it myself, yet here I was actually living it out.

"Remember we agreed that Beta would have a new delivery date of the end of the year? Yesterday's board meeting accelerated everything. You guys now need to get that final presentation ready several weeks earlier. She looked at her desk calendar. Not December, but by November 10th."

The look on my face must have said it all. "We don't have a choice," she said, her face crestfallen. I took a moment to absorb this piece of news.

"Well, you're right about it pouring. Here's something else for us to throw in the mix. I need to be with my parents for at least half a day for the next three months at least. My Mom... I have to be the one to nurse her back to health, so I'll be using up all those unused vacation days that I have."

"But what about the project?" she asked. She didn't pause a moment before interjecting, and her voice was flustered. "The stakes are high here, Bill. The board also talked again about trimming the Project Management ranks next, and they gave Nick a clear directive with a December 31st due date. His job is on the line."

*Time to make a big difference.*

"Martha, before I tell you my plans, there's something you should know about my time at RingCORE. Something happened while I was there that I haven't told you about."

Her eyes opened wide as her brown eyebrows arched. She looked almost panicked. I patted the air before continuing in a gentle "calm down" gesture.

"Before I left them, I had the opportunity to stay. They offered me a position. It's a great company, and working there would have been an awesome experience, but I discovered that I had a commitment to my friends here at Syscon. Additionally, I wanted to get us out of the rut we're in -- low productivity, poor time management, the whole thing. I wanted to bring back what I had learned -- all that stuff you heard at the meeting with Manuel and Vernon. Now, they have offered me another position. They want me to come back to a promotion."

Instantly, her face went white. It shocked me: her success was also riding on Beta, and if I left now, she'd be totally screwed.

"But I'm not going to take the job. When I committed to coming back, I struggled to let go of the fear of being laid off -- in my clearer moments -- it's simply not a concern I carry with me. That's no longer my purpose here at Syscon... to keep my job. Instead, my new job is to unlock the kind of time management methods that can change people's lives on an individual level. They can have more of what they want in all parts of their lives, simply by making consistent upgrades. Plus, if you improve individual time management, you have a more productive company. Remember that metric... 23%" "

She stared at me as if she were looking at a stranger. Before I could say anything else, a tear rolled down her cheek. It didn't last a second before she wiped it away with the back of her hand. She started to say something, but her lower lip was trembling so much that she clamped her mouth shut.

"To make sure Beta succeeds, I'm going to ask Ted to step into the project management role instead of me. He's already made tremendous strides using the 7 Ladders, and we know exactly what he needs to improve next to get even better. He's itching for something important enough, I think. His own way to make a difference."

"Ted? Are you sure he's up to this? He's gotten better, but I remember the days when he couldn't return a phone call."

I nodded. Those days were fresh in my mind also, and now... here I was putting my faith, and Martha's career, for that matter, in his hands. And hoping desperately that the improvements he had made in "Capturing" and the other ladders would keep working.

"Bill... I... I hope it works. Listen, I'll handle all the politics -- Manuel and Nick... they don't need to know." She whispered this slowly. A big risk, I knew, but we were all taking a plunge of some kind, so it fit right in.

For a moment we looked at each other, as if to cement our new partnership.

A minute later, I stopped at the balcony overlooking the atrium and called Sandy. Five minutes later, I typed out a short message to Mike with an important decision from the reconstituted "Crossley Team of Two."

"Mike, thanks for the opportunity for the promo. I'm staying put at Syscon. This is the place where I want to make a difference. Tell you more later."

Within a few minutes I got a response. "No problem, Bill. I'll tell Andre. We'll fill it from the inside. Your protégé from Phoenix is already tee'd up: she's ready and raring to go."

As I put my phone away, I felt it buzzing with a BPM message. Returning to the balcony, I saw that it was a message from Vernon. "Check your email."

There was a message from him marked "Re: Confidential Question."

*What now?*

The thread included several messages between Manuel, Martha and other managers. The most recent email was at the very top with a list of Project Managers who were being recommended for the next round of layoffs. My name appeared - Crossley, Bill - in what looked like a list whose other names had been deleted.

A surge of angry adrenalin shot through my body and I took in a sharp breath. This was it. It looked as if I was on the list of layoffs, even though it made no mention of a final announcement.

At the very top of the email, it said, "Bill, Here's the information you asked me to get. Once again, please don't let anyone know. Vernon"

I shook my head. Obviously, I never asked him to do any such thing. But it was his digital alibi - a way to cover his ass in style while claiming that it was all a misunderstanding and he would never have sent these messages if I hadn't pushed him. It was easy to see what he was doing and how he was doing it but... *Now what?*

# Chapter 15

I was pleased as punch at the job Ted was doing in the front of the room and had to suppress a huge smile so that I wouldn't come across as a jackass. He described how the Beta Team's prototype would change the way companies trained their employees using the Zebon technology, and I felt a growing sense of pride.

"Martha would feel the same way," I thought. She was missing the meeting due to an awful bout of flu, but Nick, Manuel, Vernon, and a few other senior managers were listening intently to this final presentation from the Beta team. There were even a couple of board members in attendance: a man and a woman dressed in dark, expensive suits. They were the oldest people in the room, and it was unusual to have them here: Board members at Syscon usually avoided this level of detail. But Zebon was hot and there were 25 customers from Fortune 50 companies eager to hear what we had to offer.

Ted was playing the role of project manager to the fullest. The reports from his team members were glowing. Rapidly improved time management skills made all the difference, and they were inspired to follow his example. He had earned a new nickname - "The Fireman" - for the way he had charged up the 7 Ladders and called on them to do the same. Everyone knew that his profile had changed the most, and it showed in his confidence. I would promote him on the spot to be an official Project Manager if I could.

The "Good Luck" wishes from that morning were still keeping me warm inside. Sandy gave me a big kiss as I left the house, whispering the words "Team of Two" as I gave her a long hug.

Mom and Dad called to tell me to "break a leg." Both parents had improved considerably, and my Mom was now moving around on her own, proving that my decision to spend time with them over the past two months had paid off. Even Lizzy drew a picture for me of suited managers in a meeting, along with the words "Good Luck Daddy" written at the top.

I glanced around the room to see how Ted was being received. Vernon looked tight-lipped, as usual. I had ignored his cover-my-ass email. *Asshole.*

Manuel looked quite happy, albeit a bit confused. He introduced the team to start off the meeting, handing over to me, but I passed control right over to Ted. The furrow in his brow became pronounced at that moment, and it remained in place.

Everyone else seemed intrigued, which was right where they should be. This was critically important to the company's future and needed to be taken seriously. If another company beat us to the market with a Zebon prototype, it would be a disaster.

The Fortune 50 customers looked happy to begin working with the prototype as soon as it was practically possible, and they left the room to complete the demos we had set up in another room filled with workstations. That left the Beta team and Syscon employees behind, in order to answer some questions away from the eyes of our customers.

At the end of the Q&A session, Nick spoke up. "You guys need to be congratulated. It's clear that you had to do a lot of work in a short time, and I believe it demonstrates the kind of productive methods that we need to be using to get our company to the next level. We need to close that 23 percent productivity gap, as you all know, and I think you guys have shown that it can be done."

Ted was beaming. We all were.

Vernon raised his hand with a smile on his face. When Nick nodded in his direction, he said with a cheer, "I think that it's amazing what they have done with Bill working part-time for so long. That makes it even more of a stretch."

Nick and Manuel swiveled in their chairs to look at me. "Weren't you the Project Manager, Bill?" asked Manuel.

"No," I said with a slight crack in my voice. "Ted took over back in September. He ran with this project entirely."

Nick's eyebrows shot up and Vernon's trap, so carefully couched in the form of a kudo, was sprung.

He added, "Plus, I think it was a good idea to bring in outside consultants to work with the team. The team needed that extra firepower to take it to the next level."

At this remark, Manuel actually jumped in his seat. Nick's face started changing colors, first to red, then to purple. "One at a time," he sputtered, glancing over at the two board members, who were whispering something to each other. "So... Bill... you were only working on Beta part-time." I nodded quietly. "And weren't you away at RingCORE for the better part of this year?" I nodded again. As he glanced looked over at the two board members, he took out a black notebook and wrote something with an expensive-looking pencil. The room was silent except for the sound of lead scratching away on paper.

Ted, seeing what was happening, shot out, "Hey, hold on a minute. There's no way we could have gotten to this point without Bill. He gave us the way to get better using these new ideas, plus a guy called G who trained us. He wasn't missing from the project, believe me. Without him, I wouldn't have been able to lead the project by myself. His family needed him... his Mom in particular..." His voice trailed off as he ran out of steam. I loved Ted, but the silence in the room swallowed his words.

"But at the end of the day, you managed this on your own, right Ted?" Nick's voice sounded cold. An eagle swooping down on a mouse, I imagined.

"Ahhhm, yes, you could say so, but... it's not as if we didn't need Bill... and I... I..." He couldn't finish the sentence. Ted, who always had a smart, cynical quip about anything that mattered in the office, just didn't know what to say.

"Ted, how many full-time team members did you use for this project?"

He replied, "Six."

An awkward silence fell as Nick scribbled away, and I remembered that damned study. *23%.*

"We just need to be efficient about how we use our resources around here. Going forward. "If the silence before he spoke was awkward, it was now deafening.

"And this G -- is that a firm that worked with you guys to get this done? How much of a role did they play?"

Once again, Ted jumped in. "We invited a time management expert to work with us for two days at our retreat. One guy. His intervention was critical -- we'd be nowhere without his help. Nowhere." He was so passionate and so defensive that he wasn't making sense.

*We deserve an explanation.* It was that mysterious voice speaking inside me, and before I knew it, it got me out of my chair and I walked to the front of the room. Ted sat down looking like his dog had just died, and I patted his shoulder lightly.

It was my voice now, but different. I started, "For the better part of the last eighteen months, all I tried to do was prevent myself from being laid off. Like many of you, I heard rumors about a list floating around that had all the names of people who were going to get cut. I tried to give my full attention to that list, working damned hard to make sure that the name Bill Crossley never got added to it.

"While I was away at RingCORE, I had a revelation. A company staffed with people concerned only about their survival won't last. Cutting headcounts and costs turns out to be an easy way to ensure that the least productive ones leave, raising the productivity of the company as a whole. But it starts a disease that's nearly impossible to reverse and eventually erodes the productivity of all who do stay for as long as the threat remains.

"While I was away at RingCORE, its CEO, along with a consultant named G, offered me an opportunity to contribute to their effort to make the firm more productive. As you probably know, they already have a fantastic reputation for being innovative and efficient at the same time, by any number of metrics. Any comparison with them puts our numbers in perspective -- we have a long way to go. The opportunity they gave me was a precious one, as I discovered a talent for thinking about time management in new ways. They encouraged me to continue working with them, and when I was told to report back to Syscon before the end of the contract, they asked me if I wanted to stay -- they'd work it out so that I could join RingCORE."

Nick's back stiffened and his eyebrows arched, but I kept on talking.

"But if I had stayed at RingCORE, it would have been just a gambit to save my skin. I learned that I desperately wanted my friends at Syscon to inhabit a different reality in which their productivity was not a function of cutting, but of growing. One in which fear was replaced by courage and confidence.

"So I turned down RingCORE and came back. When my parents' health took a turn for the worse and the deadlines for the Beta Team were shortened again and again, I'll tell you the truth... I was tempted to leave.

"What kept me here? What made me want to sneak in a consultant when we weren't supposed to be using them? What made me stay to contribute to the Beta Team when my parents' illness warranted full-time care? It's just because I have always imagined what it would be like to turn Syscon around -- not just its bottom line, but for its people who work here every day and want to do a good job, not one filled with fear. People who care for this company, for each other, for their families and their personal lives, but they can't translate all that caring into practical results because they believe they don't have time.

Or, as we have come to learn in the Beta Team, it's not because we don't have time. It's because our time management skills haven't been upgraded to keep up with their lives. That's where it starts, but it doesn't end there. An individual who knows how to make upgrades can always make a superior contribution, can help reverse a company's fortunes, and can find the discretionary time needed to reverse a 23% productivity deficit that returns a company to profitability.

But it starts with the individual and what he can learn to do if we only believe in him, give him our trust, and try our best to remove his fears."

I looked around the room, wanting every word to sink in, because I knew this could be one of my last meetings at Syscon.

No one said anything, so I moved back to my seat but before I could get there, Manuel broke the silence.

He still looked shocked. "I had no idea Bill was working on this part-time." I braced myself, remembering his explicit doubts about my ideas from Martha's office the last time we had spoken. This meeting wasn't supposed to go this way.

"At the same time, the only reason he could step back the way he needed to... was because he put a new approach to improving each team member's time management skills in place. I did some research on the 7 Ladders approach he's been using after it came up in one of our meetings. I was curious, so I got in touch with G, the consultant he's been working with."

He turned to me and said, "Andre Anderson and I have been personal friends since we were college roommates, and he introduced me to G about ten years ago. He filled me in on everything you guys have been working on."

Nick, the two board members, Vernon, the members of Beta... everyone leaned in closely.

"Think about it -- he set up a way for each person to upgrade their productivity so quickly that he could step away and not miss a beat as the momentum continued on its own. I understand from G that the only way for a company to move forward is to give individual employees the tools to understand their current skills and improve them. Taking a few small steps at a time is the key. This is a remarkable thing that's been done."

Vernon jumped in. "But it's not better than the Master Time Method, is it Manuel? I mean... it's way too complicated! We're all smart enough to know that."

Manuel only shook his head quietly. When he finally spoke, his accented voice was full of unspoken warning and intent directed at Vernon, who finally got the cue to shut up.

"We need more examples of what Bill has done. More managers and project managers who teach people how to get better on their own, not just how to follow a prescription. Life is too complex for pre-packaged rules. Plus, we are all too busy to play the role of policemen. Flexibility and simplicity make the 7 Ladders approach work. I don't think it's the final answer – I don't think anything is – but it includes so many key elements that match the kind of reality we live in. That's what makes it important."

Ted burst out, "There's no way I could have managed this project without getting better. If you told me that I could manage a project like this just a few months ago, I'd have said you were crazy. My skill profile went from being a white belt to a yellow belt, and I'm almost an orange."

Only a few of us understood what he meant, but his intent was clear.

Nick nodded with an appreciative look on his face that I had never seen before. "Bill, it looks like the risks you took have paid off. How quickly can we get this approach up throughout the company? The consultants told us we needed to close the gap, except that when I pushed them to tell us how, they didn't have an answer besides 'cut costs'."

I answered, "A good first step would be to share what we did in the Beta team and how we did it here at Syscon. Then, we should decide next steps. I'll set it up."

* * *

"I got through college without a time management system and haven't used one up until now. Why should I start?"

It was the first question of the morning, and Ted was standing confidently at the front of the room. His cocky smirk was missing; it was now something he used only in our private moments of kidding around.

We were in a much larger conference room, two weeks after the Fortune 50 presentation, with about 100 people. They were listening to him share the highlights of the Beta team's accomplishments in an open session. This was the first of four meetings that were planned to start with a short introduction followed by an open Q&A. Employees, managers, customers, and a couple more Board members in their usual suits sat quietly as he took the first question.

He had just praised Vernon in overly generous terms for his efforts to help boost productivity at the start of the project, effectively burying the hatchet. Vernon smiled and waved at the audience on cue. His recent email to Manuel, Martha and me had shown that MTM could be enhanced with the 7 Ladders approach. He seemed to understand the heart of the matter. It was nice, but I still viewed him as a dangerous snake. *Better to keep him close where I can see him.*

Ted echoed the question for those in the back. "The question was, what if you got through college without a time management system and haven't used one until now. Why change?" The younger, 20 something year old guy who had asked the question nodded, and I joined Ted on the stage to back him up if needed.

Ted answered like the expert he had become, "What we found is that every single person who works for a living has a system, even though he or she may not have recognized it or given it a name. As long as you have time commitments of some kind and you move them around mentally, you've got a system. It was an eye-opener for most of us to understand that we already have something that was performing well in some ways and under performing in others. That's why the first step we learned in our team was how to diagnose and understand our current methods." He was getting sharp, our Ted. *Putting up some points on the very first play.*

"But isn't it true that there's no such thing as time management?"

Jumping in to expand on one of my favorite topics, I responded, "That's quite true. It's more accurate to speak about time *demand* management. A time demand is an individual commitment to complete a task in the future. These mental creations are what we need to capture, allocate, add to a schedule, list, store, toss away and execute." He looked a bit stunned, so he asked me to repeat myself as he took out a notepad. Quite a few others started scribbling. "We manage time demands with our repetitive actions. While they are often self-taught, they do follow a particular structure."

A young lady asked, "I just attended a workshop on MTM -- how is this different?"

Ted replied, "I also attended MTM training and learned quickly that some of the ideas worked for me while others didn't. I did what everyone else does when confronted with a prescriptive set of habits that are tough to implement -- pick and choose.

"On Beta," he said, "we started at a different place. Instead of trying to get everyone to follow the same habit pattern, we helped people depict their current methods. One step at a time, we made changes to our existing systems to fit our needs. A few of our team members ended up with systems that look a lot like MTM, but that's not the end of the story for them. They'll continue to put upgrades in place so what they end up having a year from now may look very different than it does today. Anyone who wants read to MTM, and decides to implement that system of habits can benefit from this approach." *Nothing but net - he was scoring all sorts of points today.*

Ted looked at Vernon to see if he had any comment, and I could see his eyes blazing from across the room. But he looked away – he didn't challenge Ted's clear gaze in his direction.

The young lady wasn't finished, however. "Won't this just become the next thing that needs to be replaced at some point?"

This time, Ted didn't hesitate. "I hope so. Professionals need to learn how to keep upgrading their methods all the time. Life is changing so fast, driven by new technology and increasing volumes of work, that it's up to us to keep scanning the horizon for new thinking, tools, metrics -- anything we can incorporate into our lives to manage our time better. The best thing I can hope for is for people to take their development in this area seriously and never allow it to be driven by an external force."

"What about new technology? How do you handle that when it gets offered to you by a hot new company, or even by your own management?" That question came from a fellow who was close to retirement, and I decided to take it.

"I think I'd encourage someone to use our approach before purchasing new technology. That way, you know exactly what practice you're trying to improve before looking for a way to automate it.

"I purchased a smartphone last year, thinking that it would be the answer to my time management challenges. It helped a little bit... I could now send and receive messages from some very unusual places. But that was more about convenience than productivity. The bottom line here is that it makes more sense to focus on your habits, practices and rituals first and new technology second. Texting from the toilet isn't productive. 82 percent of y'all enjoy that particular convenience."

That got a short chuckle. "Our poor implementation of new technology is the reason we have policies against cell phone use while driving. Bad Habits + New Technology = Chaos."

There was another chuckle as I announced my formula, and a few people scribbled it down. *An easy lay-up.*

Martha jumped in, "Why focus on individual productivity rather than something like better teamwork?"

Ted immediately looked at me for help. We had to double team quickly to score on this one. "There is definitely a place for better teamwork and improved communication. Sometimes, however, it's all about time management, and most times it requires a little of both. I don't know which one is more important. In our case, we felt like there weren't enough hours in the day. We knew we had to boost our team's capacity to complete time demands. Each team needs to make a call about which improvements to focus on and which ones to exclude."

She added, "Was it easy to implement?"

"Unfortunately, there is no way to boost your capacity without dealing with the new habits you need to develop. It's tough to do, but changing habits lies at the core of doing most things better in the long term, whether it's a sport, an artistic endeavor, or working on new product development. In other words, you can't escape the need to change habits, practices and rituals that are the heart of most improvement efforts. This is neither easy, nor quick. Forget about tips, tricks and shortcuts."

In the front row, Nick's eyes lit up, "But why focus on the team doing this together? Isn't an improvement in your productivity only up to you?"

Ted regained his feet and answered, "It's possible to focus on improving your productivity on your own, but we found that our habits were much harder to change than we thought. We supported each other, and it became easier to keep going and finish each upgrade. We just refused to let our teammates fail, given how closely we worked and how much we wanted to succeed. Someone who works alone has a greater challenge and needs to set up a support system using electronic reminders, journals, or coaches. I can give you some great books to read on this topic that say the same thing: knowing how to change your habits, practices and rituals is more difficult than finding out what you need to change."

One of the board members raised his hand politely. "How does each person make the choice about what to change? What if they make a mistake and choose the wrong thing?"

"Good question," Ted started. "Our initial ideas of what we thought we needed to focus on were quite incorrect, and most of us had to change our plans within the first few weeks. We realized that we were novices at this game of changing habits, practices and rituals. Bill encouraged us to see it as a series of experiments, in which we'd try different upgrades and a number of support systems to see what worked. This helped us a lot, and it took the pressure off. In addition, we learned to set our own standards. We each picked an individual goal -- mine was "Reliable Efficiency" -- and measured any proposed and actual changes against that goal. If it took us closer, then it was working. If it didn't help, we changed course."

Nick asked, "I heard that you guys didn't work longer hours -- is that true?"

"There were some long days," said Ted, "but it was the exception rather than the rule. We made a joint commitment as a team to find ways to expand our capacity to deal with time demands rather than scheduling them for nights and weekends. In that way, those who worked overtime didn't have to, even if they chose to."

Our longtime CFO asked, "How can we hardwire this approach into the organization? It seems so obvious, but I don't know of any other company that follows these principles to their natural conclusion."

Ted looked at me for some reason and gestured in my direction. I said, "We can get everyone in the company trained in this approach, but I think it's better to do it either in their natural working groups or in project teams. In that way, they can start the process of upgrading their systems with help from others. I wouldn't wait to train individuals if the team approach is available."

Everyone in the room was nodding. Martha seemed particularly pleased as we took the last round of questions, just as I handed the meeting back to Nick to wrap things up.

"I want to thank the Beta Team for its leadership in this important area. What you have come up with is important not only for Syscon, but also for teams and individuals who need a commonsense way to get better for their own sake and for the company. I wish it was as easy as buying some new equipment, but I'm learning today that this is simply not the case. I want to move aggressively to set up the kind of training that Bill described, and I also want a team of mentors to work with each team. Bill, I want you to lead that up. But not as project manager. As a full manager -- we'll talk about that offline."

The room erupted in applause.

He held up his hands. "You all should remember that consultant's report on Employees' Productivity? It talked about the work we needed to do in this area. The board working with the management team has decided to delay our headcount reductions by at least a year to see if we can get improvements in the business with this approach. The truth is: we can't cut our way to greatness; we have tried that strategy without success. We do have a shot at growing our way to greatness, and that, for me, is why this approach can be great. The 7 Ladders approach is a tool we'll use to change this business one person at a time, or as these Beta guys say... one habit, practice and ritual at a time."

* * *

Nick was as good as his word.

A year later, as a fairly new manager at Syscon, I headed up a new Zebon Product Team and sat on our new Individual Productivity Council. The council's goal was to empower Syscon's employees to be more productive in all parts of their lives. The company would give them the best methods for improving their time management skills. My new team included most of the Beta team's original members. Our workspace displayed updated charts with our current belts and the habits we were working to change. My progress towards a Green Belt was still not complete: it was moving only in fits and starts. I knew how stubborn habits could be and the gains at this point were slower in coming than they were in the beginning. G had warned me about this.

Already existing teams were given the option of being trained first, but the clamor became so loud that we also began offering classes for 20 people at a time.

As the lead designer and one of the instructors, I discovered that our staff was largely interested in increasing the number of time demands they could handle in full and often the reasons had nothing to do with Syscon. They wanted to lead balanced, full lives, and getting better seemed to give them the chance to have more of what they wanted. Some wanted to be promoted. Others wished for more time with their kids or in their communities. It was all up to the individual, and we trusted that regardless of their initial motivation for improvement, in the end, Syscon would benefit.

Fortunately, the company's numbers were now all headed in the right direction. Profitability and overall productivity were all up. It was hard to quantify the role that individual productivity played, but HR did a study of employee Tzinbox scores and found a strong correlation with company performance. A part of the study showed that the Beta team's Tzinbox scores, had made us the fastest improving work group in the corporation, even though we had never paid any attention to them.

Syscon's flexible working policy turned out to be ideal for a great number of employees, especially for people like me who needed to manage an unorthodox schedule. It helped us take full advantage of the company's wisdom, but eventually the Human Resource Department decided to make our time management training a prerequisite for going on flex time.

As for Vernon, he remained in love with MTM, but he told everyone who would listen that "The Master Time Method was a critical milestone in the development of the 7 Ladders." I didn't contradict his version of events. Not publicly anyway. Only Ted and Sandy heard my true feelings about Vernon and the Stevnellie email he had sent.

At a private thank-you dinner for G, the original Beta team had a chance to thank him for his help and for quietly saving all of our careers from ruin. The 7 Ladders approach went to RingCORE, where they would also use his ideas. He was equally thankful for the challenge we had thrown in his lap, and he told us quietly that Andre insisted on the latest stuff. "I have renamed the Ladders, by the way. They are now known as the 'fundamentals.' Also, I have 4 Advanced Fundamentals - Switching, Interrupting, Warning and Reviewing, plus another new one on the way. Some of you people might lose a belt or two after learning about the new stuff that you need to master!" Ted started running out of the restaurant in a mock-panic, startling G, who had forgotten about "our Ted." We all laughed out loud, causing people to stare at us, which only made us laugh harder.

When he got over his shock, G added, "We are also working on some software: a tool to manage time demands. Not email, tasks or schedules. Time demands." He emphasized the last phrase slowly, as if to underline its importance. No-one dared ask for details, but I promised myself to bend his ear in private.

Mom was now walking freely after using a crutch and then a cane for about seven months. She was almost back to full health, due in no small part to the quality time I was able to devote to both parents' care. Things hadn't gone as well for my Dad, who remained sickly, but stable - no better or worse. As a result, they both moved into my place and we rented out their house. Adding a new room in the back for them made all the difference. Thank goodness the refinanced mortgage on our home went through without a hitch, and the suffering from crazy interest rates was over.

In the grand scheme of things, having Sandy back in my life was one of the most important gifts I received from the project. It was kind of ironic. I returned to Syscon to try to make a big difference, but didn't realize that I would be one of the biggest beneficiaries. Andre and G could tell from our now monthly calls, and so could Sandy. All was well, but more importantly, it was on its way to getting even better. *Perfect.*

# Where to Go Next

Thanks for reading *Bill's Im-Perfect Time Management Adventure*. Please share your impressions of the book with an Amazon Review, a share on Facebook, or a Tweet. We are also on Goodreads.

*December 2014 Update*: You can learn more about my new book on page 199. It's called *Perfect Time-Based Productivity*.

If I have done my job well as an author, then you probably have a number of questions that you didn't have before you flipped open this book. If you belong to one of the following groups, follow the appropriate links to specific pages on http://perfect.mytimedesign.com to learn more about further learning opportunities that follow what I call "The Bill Book."

An Experienced, Productive Professional (a defacto Lifehacker)
Bill, Ted and Mike might be more like you: people who want to get better because they either love the experience of learning or simply want practical results that improve on the past. If you like to do that kind of work on yourself to make things better, then
visit http://perfect.mytimedesign.com/mike-nutz.

Executive, Entrepreneur or Type-A Businessperson
Martha, Andre and Vernon all wanted practical business results, and like you they sometimes get impatient as they wait to get them. Your attention is on the bottom line so you want to get dramatic improvements in your performance as quickly as possible. Waste no time in checking
out http://perfect.mytimedesign.com/executive.

Coach, Consultant, Trainer or Professional Organizer
Like G, you advise working adults on how to improve their time management or time clutter skills. Visit http://perfect.mytimedesign.com/g-coaching to find out how to improve your own performance as an adviser, use content from the book with your clients, and one day get qualified as a Certified Time Management Adviser (CTMA.)

Project or Team Manager
Like Bill, your job is to supervise other people who (you hope) are improving their time management skills so that they keep up with a tough job or challenging project. Getting them into the kaizen frame of mind can be a challenge, but you can find some answers here:
http://perfect.mytimedesign.com/bill-as-pm.

Training and Development Professional
Unfortunately, Syscon didn't have someone in this role due to its lack of progressive thinking. Nevertheless, RingCORE's HR Lab showed strong signs that some pretty smart people were behind the scenes, and they turned Andre's ideas into on-the-ground programs and interventions. You are someone with a similar role, and you can get some help at: http://perfect.mytimedesign.com/train-and-dev-admin.

Academic Researcher
You are one of the handful of researchers in the world with an interest in a field that's critical to every single business person, every single day, but has no real home in academia. The source of the ideas that underlie The Bill Book may interest you. If you can't wait for my next book, then visit: http://perfect.mytimedesign.com/g-as-academic.

***New (December 2014)***

I have also started developing resources for content developers who focus on time management. If you are a blogger, podcaster, tweeter, author, video-maker or Pinner you may benefit from the latest science and how it's changing the face of time-based productivity. Follow this link: http://wp.me/PeenO-H0

Also, if you are a developer of time management tools (hardware, software or paper) then you may be interested in joining others in my private mailing list. Visit http://goo.gl/S4gLbf and sign up to receive updates or simply join my Google community at http://goo.gl/6yD9SP.

If none of these categories apply to you, simply visit the pages that you find the most interesting, and come visit the reader's discussion forum at http://perfect.mytimedesign.com/forums.

My Contact Information
Email: http://ReplytoFrancis.info
Twitter: @fwade
Facebook: https://www.facebook.com/2timepage
Phone: 1-305-647-3770
Address: 3389 Sheridan Street, No. 434, Hollywood FL 33021, USA

# A Time Management 2.0 Summary

*This isn't your parents' time management! In fact, it starts with the understanding that <u>time can't be managed</u> at all, but you can influence and transform your habits, practices and rituals.*
Using Time Management 2.0 is all about following these guidelines:

- **Refusing** to play "follow the leader." Give up on trying to squeeze someone else' one-size-fits-all-perfectly-defined-prescription-for-productivity into your busy, chaotic life.
- **Recognizing** that you already have your own way of managing your time. Use it as a starting point for any changes you make. It cannot be ignored.
- **Knowing** that you are unique and always will be. Therefore, you need a tailored system that suits your lifestyle, culture, idiosyncrasies and comfort with technology.
- **Giving** yourself a perpetual upgrade path and appreciating that today's cool methods quickly become tomorrow's stale rituals.
- **Being** realistic. Decide to make some changes, and know that even the best-intentioned adopt new habits slowly. The best way to implement even a major upgrade is one habit at a time and a feasible plan should take your full human nature into account.

# Acknowledgements

*Dedicated to my wife, parents, family and friends. For your patience.*

My wife Dale has been my biggest supporter throughout the writing of this book, and she deserves my warmest gratitude. Without her, it's likely that none of this would have happened, including our move to live in Jamaica: the creative spark that inspired this book.

Thanks also to my parents, Barry and Merle, plus friends, colleagues and clients who all put my ideas to the test over the years and encouraged me even when they didn't quite work out as planned. It's taken them great patience.

The content of this book did not come from my working alone. I'd like to thank all the working professionals with whom I have interacted over the years for sharing the truth about their time-based challenges. Their honesty and authenticity challenged me to dig deeper until I could find the kind of answers that could begin to make a difference, even when they seemed far removed from time management.

While hundreds of people have taken my training in different formats, I'd like to recognize the handful who were willing to help or critique the ideas put forth in my published content and training programs. It only makes sense to write a book on time management after a number of people have tested its ideas and found them useful. They may not have realized that they were "writing" a book in the process, but here we are!

I often complain that time management is not sufficiently researched, but I must praise and acknowledge those who have completed research in this field. Their work has provided a critical foundation of ideas I used in this book. I can only thank them and ask that they keep going. Too many basic questions remain unanswered.

Writing a novel may come easily to some, but in my case, it certainly did no such thing. Engineers only pursue this path when nothing else seems to work, a problem I described in the Preface. My copy-editor, Ellen Fishbein, helped me actually enjoy the process from start to finish. She was insightful, but also warm-hearted and gracious. Thanks also to my substantive editor, Desiree Starr, for her early input and solid encouragement.

A small army of beta-testing editors played an indispensible role by volunteering to read and suggest improvement to the book before publication. Those include: Andrew Yee, Barry Wade, Bianca Welds, Colleen Dupont, Dale Pilgrim Wade, Glen E. Sharp, Jay Carter, Joyce Kristjansson, Judith Morrain Webb, Katrina Prince Burell, Karen Schoch McDaniel, Keith Ford, LaRonda Robinson, Layla Brown, Marcia Jean Oxley, Megan Smoot, Nicki Franklin-Grant, Rhoda Williams-Moore, Robin Blanc, Sarah Buerger, Stanley Nicholls, Stephanie N. Cain, Suzi Ure, Tom Jansen and Trudy Myers Edwards.

Also, a number of individuals gave me important information based on their experience: Denise Mathews, Raj Venugopal and all the members of the InnerLab.

Francis

2Time Labs
http://perfect.mytimedesign.com

# Just Released

When I started writing *Bill's Imperfect Time Management Adventure* (The Bill Book), I envisioned a three part series, of which this is the first. In November 2014, I released the second book entitled *Perfect Time-Based Productivity: A unique way to protect your peace of mind as time demands increase.*

At the end of The Bill Book, Andre Anderson, the CEO of RingCORE, was about to launch a program within the company to help teach individual employees how to upgrade their way of managing time. Little did he know that a notion he had entertained (that time could not actually be managed) would play a big role in teaching his people a realistic way to improve their skills.

Perfect Time-Based Productivity pulls together the contents of that program, providing a step-by-step method. It comprehensively covers the science behind the 7 Essential and 4 Advanced Fundamentals and mentions a possible $5^{th}$ Fundamental under consideration. All the charts, tables and forms that you need to start transforming your time management system into an evergreen, dynamic one plus all the academic and internet references are included. http://perfect.mytimedesign.com

**The Art and Science of Time Management Advising** (*a working title*)
Due to Syscon's budgetary constraints, G played an abbreviated role as the Beta Team's adviser. Consultants, coaches, professional organizers and trainers in time management often develop more lasting relationships with their clients due to the span of time required to effect an upgrade. This book will give you, a professional adviser in this field, a framework to work with your clients that will dramatically improve your effectiveness.

For early notification about future publications, visit the following page, and I'll let you know when they become available:
http://perfect.mytimedesign.com/earlybook.

www.ingramcontent.com/pod-product-compliance
Lightning Source LLC
Chambersburg PA
CBHW071425170526
45165CB00001B/405